# JENNIE P

MW00851157

# THE WORK BOOK

# Self Sabotage No More

## LEARN HOW TO IDENTIFY & RELEASE

What's Holding You Back and Align to What
You Want in Fifteen Minutes a Day

THIS WORKBOOK BELONGS TO

_____

ISBN: 979-8-9866007-1-0

Cover Design and Interior Layout by Margaret Cogswell Designs

This work is dedicated to Dave Potter,
my husband and best friend, who
encourages me, aligns with me,
and grows with me everyday.

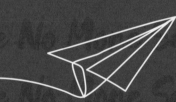

# Welcome to
## YOUR WORKBOOK

# EVER FELT "STUCK" BUT DON'T KNOW WHY?

Procrastinate for no sane reason? Constantly overthink things? Feel like you are never good enough? Have a persistent, underlying feeling of guilt? Or, simply not living up to your full potential? You want to make a change. Build your business, make more money, lose that extra weight ... you vow that tomorrow you are going to make it happen! But tomorrow comes and you don't get started, or even if you do get started, some hidden force keeps you from fully committing. **In short, you sabotage yourself.**

Based on my book, *Self Sabotage No More*, I have created this workbook to help you learn how to reset your autopilot destination, reframe your filter, identify unprocessed emotions, sabotage beliefs, and limiting sabotage setpoints around wealth, health, relationships, and more.

Over the past few years, I have been obsessed with discovering why people set goals, but then get in their own way. What I discovered are a few consistent variables that affect everyone. Everyone creates an autopilot setting before the age of 12; depending on who helped you program your autopilot, your destination might include statements like: I'm not worthy of success, I'm not smart enough to succeed, I'll never be happy, I'll never fit in, I'm not wanted, or I'm not special.

Additionally, we have a function or filter called the Reticular Activating System (RAS). This collects proof to keep you in line with your autopilot settings and sabotage beliefs.

And the last major variable, which I cover in my book, *Self Sabotage No More*, are emotions that get stuck in processing. This workbook is designed to help you reset your autopilot, release your sabotage beliefs, collect proof for a new filter setting, and

*As a child I was an "emotional sponge". I always had the ability to "see" people's feelings and emotions I also took them on as my own. I had trouble processing emotions and they would get stuck in what I call the emotional body.*

release any unprocessed emotions which are causing you to sabotage. In the back of this workbook are 15 Minute Daily Exercises that will help you release and identify emotions, sabotage beliefs, and set points that cause you to self sabotage.

Some of what we will cover in this journey together is:
- Why your "autopilot" reaction is often to self-sabotage and how to reset your autopilot destination
- What is your sabotage filter and how you can change it?
- The role your energy and vibration play in self-sabotage and how to reduce the negative noise and align with your true vibration and purpose.
- Why and how emotions get "stuck" in processing and how to release them.
- How to identify and release "sabotage setpoints" that limit every area of your life
- A specific process called the ALARM method for releasing and resetting sabotage emotions and beliefs
- How to move forward after identifying, releasing, resetting, and aligning.

It's time to start your journey of releasing the triggers that hold you back. Get ready to step into a brand new life, into your divine mission, where you *Self Sabotage No More!*

*Videos will accompany the workbook throughout and you can access those on YouTube @JenniePotterFirekeeper*

## - JENNIE POTTER

*"You are divine. It's time to start being that. Quit pretending you're not."*
*PAMELA WILSON*

Check out my videos on how to release Sabotaging Beliefs!

7

# PRAISE FOR SELF SABOTAGE NO MORE

I had already done a lot of mindset work. I knew I needed something more. Working with Jennie not only helped me unblock and release unprocessed emotions but we also discovered patterns together. My entire team is now working with Jennie.
KIMBERLY OLSON
*Best Selling Author, Speaker, and CEO of Goal Digger Girl Co.*

Before working with Jennie and releasing unprocessed emotions I felt stuck and overwhelmed. I went from one to two clients a month to 3+ clients weekly.
GEMMA SHARPE
*Founder and CEO of Hummingbird Life Academy*

My results had been up and down. Since working with Jennie, I have tools on hand to shift more quickly, my self-talk has improved greatly, and my results are now more consistent.
JENNIE SPARKE
*Leader and Entrepreneur*

Jennie Potter helped me release 1906 unprocessed emotions. Working with her has helped me so much. I can't say I fully understand how it works but I can tell you I feel better, physically, lighter, less stressed, more peaceful. Her methods and techniques have been instrumental in helping me breakthrough my past once and for all.
RAY HIGDON
*Best selling Author, Speaker, and CEO/Founder of the Higdon Group*

I don't recommend people lightly. Jennie is a truly gifted healer and helps people move forward in a bigger bolder way. She helps people make a greater impact in the world.
CHRISTINA WHITELY
*Entrepreneur and CEO of Life Transformed*

I feel incredibly blessed to have connected with Jennie in this lifetime. Her ability to hold space for me to access and acknowledge trapped emotions in my body is truly life-changing. She has provided me with tools to be more present with how I feel and to empower myself in moments of despair.
CANDACE TRANTER
*Elite Performance Coach, Healer, Speaker, and Founder of the Dragonfly EFFECT Quest*

Working with Jennie has been amazing! When I first met her I had achieved a lot of success in my business but felt a lack of inspiration. Since working with her my creative focus has multiplied, I find so much joy in my day and feel more at peace in every area of my life.
NICOLE MONTEZ
*Entrepreneur, Founder of the BFFlife*

Working with Jennie helped me release unprocessed emotions and old sabotage beliefs which were holding me back. Since working with her, I have more clarity around my divine mission and feel more equipped to set goals and hit them.
MICHELLE BARNES
*Global Entrepreneur and Speaker/Thought Leader*

Working with Jennie has been not only been eye opening but transformative. While working with her, we have cleared and eliminated many limiting beliefs that I was holding onto. We also cleared unprocessed emotions that were holding me back. I have done MANY programs and coached with many individuals, but I feel like working with Jennie I was able to collapse the time frame to get results quicker than I ever have before. I wanted to reach a cashflow goal of $20,000 in a month, and after working with Jennie for just under 2 months, I achieved over $27,000! Her coaching, insight, and perspective are invaluable and she truly cares about her client's success. If you have the opportunity to work with her, DO IT!
KRYSTAN SAMANIEGO
*Creator of MORE to Motherhood, Financial Educator, and Published Author*

READY TO END YOUR CYCLE OF

# Self Sabotage

AND RELEASE, RESET, & ALIGN WITH WHO YOU WERE BORN TO BE?

LET'S GO OVER THE PROCESS FIRST...

# Learn to use
## YOUR CORE SKILLS

## INTRODUCTION TO CORE SKILLS

Welcome to this 15-minute daily exploration of discovering hidden obstacles, the reasons behind your self-sabotage, and how to step fully into your divine mission and shine how you were designed to!

This journey and workbook are designed to complement but stand alone from my book Self Sabotage No More. We will explore tangible tools and "how-to's" on a deeper dive to uncover your divine gifts and mission!

The first section will lay the foundation for the following daily identifications, releases, and resets. You will learn to use the tools needed to release and remove obstacles that have been holding you back. We will start with the ALARM METHOD, and work through tools such as muscle testing, discovering how many unprocessed emotions you have, identifying and releasing emotions, sabotaging beliefs, and resetting setpoints! All of these processes and more help you align with your true vibration, who you were born to be.

In the following segments, we will have daily check-ins. We will explore possible personal obstacles around health, wealth, relationships, and so much more. To have the best results in this workbook, take a moment right now to commit to some time each day to work towards this goal.

**Join the Facebook group SELF SABOTAGE NO MORE and post your progress using the hashtag #ssnm**

## COMMIT 15 MINUTES A DAY (AT THE SAME TIME EVERYDAY) TO DOING THE DAILY ACTIVITY.

*STOP* right this second, close your eyes, and picture yourself in action; picture the journey complete! Picture yourself telling someone about how you showed up every day and had transformational results. Imagine what it feels like to get out of your own way. How would your life be different? Write out your experience as if it is complete and you have achieved your goals.

## I STARTED MY JOURNEY BECAUSE I...

*Example: was procrastinating, wasn't hitting goals, felt stuck, wanted to find my divine mission, want to make more money, lose weight, feel better, not be scared to shine, etc.*

## AND NOW I AM...

*Example: in action, hitting goals, in flow with my life, clear on my mission, have increased my finances, sleeping better, feel less triggered emotionally, love myself more am more excited to shine.*

The premise behind this entire healing journey is that you are holding onto unprocessed emotions and limiting beliefs that are holding you back from your true potential. This is causing you to be out of alignment with your true self and purpose. We will cover the how of all of this in the coming weeks including the release and reset of these hidden obstacles.

We will start with the foundational and simple tool of dealing with emotions in the moment.

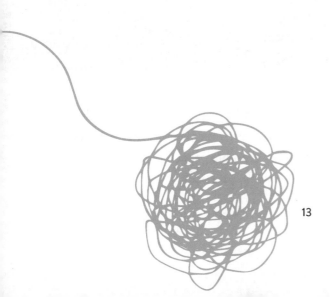

## THE ALARM METHOD

The first thing to be aware of when it comes to releasing repressed, unprocessed, pent-up emotions is that it doesn't have to be a long, drawn-out process. This can be as easy as letting air out of a blow-up mattress. Instant.

This instantaneous release is natural and how it is meant to be. Emotions are meant to alert us that something is up and then they are supposed to rise up and out. Where we get stuck is when we resist, tense up and accidentally hold on to that which doesn't feel good. We mess with the natural process by resisting or pushing down. This happens when we are not able to express our emotions and we learn what is acceptable and not acceptable. Imagine a float tied to an anchor underwater. That's your trapped emotion. Time to cut the rope. Let it rise. Picture a balloon floating away when you release it. It is that easy. Once we have identified a trapped emotion, if we want to let it go once and for all, we need to welcome it, relax into it, "unpack it," and just like that, it will release. Contrary to popular belief, hitting pillows and yelling does not release emotions; it rather exacerbates them, keeps them stuck, strengthens them, and continues to light up the old original repressed ones.

The trick is to welcome rather than avoid, expand rather than contract, to open up and release instead of tightening the grip. Sounds easy in theory... but how? I have creat-

> This can be as easy as letting air out of a blow-up mattress.
> Instant. This instantaneous release is natural and
> how it is meant to be.

ed a five-step method for you to release unprocessed emotions. You can use this the moment you experience a strong emotion or to access past emotions that got stuck in processing. I call this The Alarm Method, and it is a simple process you can use effectively and efficiently to release the stuff that's holding you back.

It stands for...
- A - AWARENESS
- L - LOCATE THE FEELING
- A - ASK YOURSELF THE QUESTION
- R - RELEASE
- M - MANTRA

# HOW TO USE THE ALARM METHOD

### Awareness of the feeling /thought /belief
This part is key. Notice what you are feeling (irritated, sad, frustrated, anxious) or when you are having negative thoughts.

### Locate the feeling
Where are you feeling it in your body (stomach, chest, head, knees)? There is no right or wrong answer here, but we always feel our emotions in our body. That's how we know we are feeling them. Locating will help you release and increase awareness for future.

### Ask yourself...
"When have I felt this before?" If nothing comes to mind, it's okay; just go to the next step. If something does pop up (even if it seems random), be curious about it and acknowledge it.

### Release
Allow the feeling to expand. Unwittingly, we resist bad-feeling emotions, and whatever you resist, persists. So, allow, not tensing but relaxing into. Use the unpacking method by moving your hand from shoulder to wrist several times, repeating the intention of releasing that emotion/belief.

Notice what it feels like and allow. Breathe in through your nose and out through your mouth 5-10 times. The emotion and all the thoughts attached to it releases like steam from a pot. It's that simple!

### Mantra

Pick something to replace the bad feelings/thoughts/beliefs (ie. I am safe, I am in action, I am awesome, I am brave, I am worthy, I am at peace). You can pack that in with intention and the shoulder to wrist movement.

This Alarm Method is from the book, *Self Sabotage No More*, by Jennie Potter.

 Check out my video on how to use the Unpacking Method

## MUSCLE TESTING & HOW TO USE IT

Another powerful method that anyone can use to identify unprocessed emotions is muscle testing and it's easy to learn.

Simply put, muscle testing is a safe, natural method of analyzing the body's needs using the body's reflexes. Muscle testing is biofeedback from the body. Everyone and everything is made up of energy, this is a way to tap into the body's energetic field—a way to speak to the subconscious.

Manual muscle testing has been used for over 60 years by doctors and physical therapists to evaluate muscle function. In the 1960s, Dr. George Goodheart used muscle testing to diagnose meridian, nerve, and muscle energy function and connections. More than just a diagnostic procedure, his discoveries led to the creation of a new system of assessment and healing that we know as applied kinesiology. I've been using muscle testing for years to determine which supplements work best for me and with other simple "yes/no" questions.

> "How the body responds can give us clues on what is stuck and what needs to heal."

Muscle testing can be used for communicating directly with the body and the subconscious. This is a skill that can come in super handy for choosing supplements, books to read, deciphering truth in a statement or situation, grocery shopping choices, and of course, for our purposes on our healing journey: identifying sabotage beliefs, unprocessed emotions, and limiting setpoints. In addition to assessing the strength of our muscle's response, we can assess the body's energetic response to questions regarding biochemical, electromagnetic, physical, emotional, and mental responses.

## HOW TO MUSCLE TEST

There are many ways to muscle test, everything from snapping your fingers, moving your hand across a surface, using a pendulum, and many more. The sway test (explained below) is my favorite for its simplicity, but feel free to search for the way that works best for you.

### Sway Test

Stand up tall with your feet pointing directly forward, hip-width apart. Make sure they're not turned slightly in or out.

Relax your body and keep your arms down by your side. Notice how you sway ever so slightly even as you stand still. To begin, you need to ask a foundational question to check for accuracy.

Don't just read this.
STAND UP! TRY THIS RIGHT NOW!

- Speak your correct name out loud. My name is _____.
- Now tune into the movement of your body.
- Speak a false name out loud. My name is _____.

Again, tune into the movement of your body. Think about it this way, you lean into and towards truth positivity, and you fall away from negativity and deceit. At this moment, look for which way your body sways. Now that you are tuned in to your body's movement, you can ask "yes/no" questions to continue using the sway test. Be mindful of the response of your body to each statement. You should feel yourself gently pulled forward for a correct response, a "yes" or pushed back indicating it's not true or your body is not in resonance with that, which would be a "no" response.

For example:
- Am I still holding on to anger from my friend "unfriending me"?
- If you get a "yes", then you can continue to ask deeper, more specific questions like, "Can I release this anger? Do I have other emotions tied to this experience?"

### *Things to Be Aware of*

Several variables can affect muscle testing results. It is important to create your base test and use "yes or no "questions. Keeping a neutral mind is ideal. Don't wear a hat, it seems to skew the results. Being hydrated is also important as hydration can affect the body's ability to optimally conduct accurate nervous system feedback. Other possible interferences could be drugs, alcohol, reaction to diet, stress, fatigue, blood sugar, etc. Always start with your base test and go from there so you know you are getting an accurate reading. The best example is using your real and then a false name.

Additionally, I always begin my sessions for myself and when working with clients by setting an intention for the highest good to come of the session. I include prayer and ask God for assistance. Although this is not a necessary step for muscle testing, it has become part of my process. The work feels nothing short of miraculous. I am grateful to God for the healing that occurs and the gift of muscle testing to communicate with our bodies so that we may clear what has been holding us back.

## FIND YOUR UPE SCORE USING MUSCLE TESTING

# WHAT IS A "UPE SCORE"?

This is the amount of unprocessed emotions you have stuck in your body. The goal is to give you the skills to release these until your score is zero! How? Muscle test to see how many unprocessed emotions you have.

Using a simple yes and no format, ask do I have more than X amount of unprocess emotions (yes or no), or do I have less than X amount of unprocessed emotions (yes or no). I muscle-tested to see how many unprocessed emotions I had and bingo, I had 496 of them to be exact! I loved knowing this because, although it seemed like a lot, it gave me something tangible to work towards.

To determine your UPE, simply start by asking, "Do I have more than 250 unprocessed emotions?" (The average adult has around 250 so starting here makes sense.) If you get a no, then ask, "Do I have more than 100?" If you get a yes, then ask again, "Is it more than 150?" Continue to ask until you land on the number. I have seen scores as few as five and as many as 2500. This is a process of elimination, so work your way to your number.

Check out my video on how to Muscle Test your UPE Score!

I started with:

_____

unprocessed emotions!

Now, we are going to watch it decrease over the coming weeks! To date, using this identification and release method I have personally helped people release thousands of emotions. *I'd love to hear about your progress. Post your UPE score and how many emotions you have released using the hashtag #UPEscore on social media!*

## RELEASE UPE'S WITH THE UNPACKING METHOD

# LET'S GET RID OF UNPROCESSED EMOTIONS!

The next step is to start releasing your unprocessed emotions using my unpacking method.

 Check out my video on how to use the Unpacking Method

You can go through the following list of emotions to see if you have that emotion stuck somewhere from a past event. You can use muscle testing to see if you cleared the emotion or not.

This may be the missing piece for you. It was for me. After I released all of my trapped emotions, I saw a dramatic change in the way I showed up daily. I was less reactive, more loving, more me, more focused, and had increased empathy for myself and others. I noticed more clearly what was mine and, more importantly, what was not. I stopped procrastinating, stopped getting migraines, gained back my energy, and faced the day differently. See my list in the coming pages of the most common low vibration emotions. You can start at the top and ask, "Do I have (insert emotion) to release?"

*Here Is An Overview Of The Process At A Glance:*
- Use muscle testing to identify or confirm unprocessed emotions.
- Use the unpacking method to release what you find.
- Muscle test to see if the emotion was released (if not, repeat unpacking movement until cleared).

*Alternatively, you can also use the ALARM method to identify and release.

EXAMPLE:
- Muscle test.
- Then ask, "Do I have unprocessed anger to release?" Yes.
- "Can I release it?" Yes.
- Release it with the unpacking method.

OR
- "Do I have unprocessed anger to release?" Yes.

- "Can I release it?" No.
- "Do I need to know more?" Yes. (You can know more by finding where in the body the emotion is, or ask intuitive questions, or check what age it first occurred.)
- Is the anger unprocessed located on: intuitive guess OR divide the body into quadrants (left side, right side, above hips, below hips).
- "Can I release the anger now?" Yes.
- Use the unpacking method to release.
- Continue, "Do I have any more to release today?" Yes.
- Keep going through the list of emotions.
- "Do I have any more to release today?" No.
- End for the day, start again next week.

Once an emotion is released, it is gone for GOOD! So congratulations! Your UPE score just got lower. NOTE: you may have unprocessed anger (or any other emotion ) multiple times from different events. Continue by asking, "Do I have any other anger that is ready to be released?" Release what your body will allow and do this exercise once a week

TIP: Each night give your subconscious the instructions to release any emotion that is willing to be released while you sleep! It is amazing what your body can do for your while your conscious mind rests. This will speed up your release time and most people see their UPE score dramatically change with the addition of this intention.

## LIST OF EMOTIONS

powerlessness

unworthiness

depression

insecurity

anxiety

despair

grief

shame

pride

worry

discouragement

disappointment

vulnerability

humiliation

unsupported

trauma/shock

jealousy

blame

anger

rage

unappreciated

overwhelm

frustration

irritation

impatience

pessimism

boredom

doubt

guilt

Note: After this exercise, you will have space for writing the details of your released emotions and/or stories around them. Go ahead and try releasing an emotion right now! Write your experience with this exercise using the lines below.

_____

_____

_____

_____

_____

_____

_____

_____

_____

_____

_____

_____

## IDENTIFY & RELEASE SABOTAGING BELIEFS

Look at the following list of common sabotage beliefs on the next page (also known as limiting beliefs or false beliefs) and muscle test the following list. If you still have not mastered muscle testing, you can use the ALARM method and notice where you feel each statement.

If you are unsure of any, mark them as a "yes." If you are using muscle testing, you can test each statement with the question, "Do I have this sabotage belief?"

As you have identify your sabotage beliefs, you can release them with the unpacking method. This is three sweeping movements, shoulder to wrist, on each arm. Include a new mantra that is the opposite of the sabotage belief you are releasing. For example, say the sabotage belief is, "I'll never be accepted." Unpack that with six sweeping movements. As a bonus, you can do the unpacking movement again and replace it with a new mantra, such as, "I am always accepted." Now, reset your filter to search for proof of what you want to see. In the example of, "I am accepted," you could grab a pen and paper and brainstorm all of the ways you are accepted. Where are the areas you are included and welcome? You want to reset your filter to notice and let in where you are accepted.

## OVERVIEW OF THE PROCESS AT A GLANCE:

- Use muscle testing to identify or confirm sabotage beliefs.
- Use the unpacking method to release what you find.
- Use the packing method to replace those with a new mantra. (The packing method is same action as unpacking with different intention.)
- Muscle test to see if the emotion/sabotage belief was released.

*Alternatively, you can use the ALARM method to identify and release.

Check out my videos on how to release Sabotaging Beliefs!

## COMMON SABOTAGE BELIEFS

I am worthless

I am ugly

The world is unsafe

I don't deserve love

I'll never be loved

I hate myself

I don't have control

I don't deserve forgiveness

I'm not worthy of respect

I'm stuck

I'm trapped

I destroy everything

I'm all alone

I'll never be accepted

I'm not enough

I'm broken/unfixable

There's not enough

There's not enough time

I'm an imposter

I'm dangerous

I'm out of control

I'm a mess

I'm stupid

Everything is dangerous/scary

I shouldn't exist

I don't belong

I'll never catch up/I'm behind

There's no point in trying

I never win

I'm not important

I'm too old

Everyone else's needs are more important

Growth is painful

Wealth is hard

Money is bad

I have to earn love

I'm weak

I'm not a priority

People will betray me

Making money is stressful

I can't have it all

If I shine, others get hurt

Every day you can release sabotage beliefs using the 15 Minute Daily Exercises at the back of the workbook. We will ask you to write out the Sabotaging Beliefs you cleared each day and a New Mantra to pack in. Go ahead and try it now using the lines below!

I identified and released this Sabotage Belief today:

_____

_____

## WHAT DID I LEARN?

This is all about reflection! We will leave you plenty of room for writing and reflecting on the following questions:

- What have I learned so far?
- What did I identify as the loudest emotions and limiting beliefs that are affecting how I show up daily?
- What am I looking forward to?
- It would be amazing if at the end of this journey I am...

## RESETTING SABOTAGE SET POINTS

How do we assess, release, and reset Sabotage Set Points and what are they? Sabotage Set Points are the limits (ceilings) that we intentionally or unintentionally set around what we believe is possible. This includes categories such as happiness, having it all, relationship contentedness, finances, physical health, spirituality, success, career, etc. Please keep in mind that through trial and error, I have discovered this works best when you have already completely cleared your UPE score and your sabotage beliefs.

As a coach and someone who works with clients using these techniques, the most frequently requested sessions I get are for resetting physical weight and financial set points. The best part (and why I wrote this workbook) is you can absolutely do this on your own. On the following page is a chart that you can use in conjunction with muscle testing to check your "set point" number out of 99. This will give you an idea of how much you need to improve in each category, with 99 being your highest score.

This might feel like magic, but it's merely shifting your mind and energy to "reset" and accept a new level in whichever category you choose. The chart is useful for your over-all scale, and I have left space for you to fill in your own categories as needed.

You can also reset specific numbers such as metabolic setpoints and financial ceilings you can't seem to break through. Use the "unpacking" movement we discussed earlier

| LIFE CATEGORY | CURRENT SET POINT | RESET | RESET | RESET | RESET | RESET | RESET |
|---|---|---|---|---|---|---|---|
| HEALTH | /99 | /99 | /99 | /99 | /99 | /99 | /99 |
| FAMILY | /99 | /99 | /99 | /99 | /99 | /99 | /99 |
| FINANCES | /99 | /99 | /99 | /99 | /99 | /99 | /99 |
| CAREER | /99 | /99 | /99 | /99 | /99 | /99 | /99 |
| HAVING IT ALL | /99 | /99 | /99 | /99 | /99 | /99 | /99 |
| HAPPINESS | /99 | /99 | /99 | /99 | /99 | /99 | /99 |
| | /99 | /99 | /99 | /99 | /99 | /99 | /99 |
| | /99 | /99 | /99 | /99 | /99 | /99 | /99 |
| | /99 | /99 | /99 | /99 | /99 | /99 | /99 |
| | /99 | /99 | /99 | /99 | /99 | /99 | /99 |
| | /99 | /99 | /99 | /99 | /99 | /99 | /99 |
| | /99 | /99 | /99 | /99 | /99 | /99 | /99 |

to reset your sabotage setpoint. Do this movement three times, then muscle test to see if it is reset. As you work on shifting your categories, you can also pick a specific topic and number and work with it.

This chart is a suggestion of categories, but there are many subjects you can use this exercise with. Metabolic setpoints, personal growth, savings, etc. The point is, you can choose your categories, these are just to get you started.

I personally used this technique when I was at a standstill with my weight after a surgery. My old set point sat between 145–150 pounds. My new set point? Stuck at 180.

For 18 months, no movement. Then I tried a reset. At first, I tried to reset it back to 145 from 180. It did not stick. Then I tried increments and it started to work better. For some people, larger increments work. For others (like me) it is one pound at a time. As I write this I have been releasing about 1 pound a week, slow and steady. I reset to 179, then 178, 177, etc. This works. I changed nothing else, have released 10 pounds, and am still dropping.

So, with your new muscle testing abilities, you can reset your weight set point. First, ask the question, "Is my weight set point higher than or lower than ___?" Then the next question is, can I reset to (put in your desired healthy weight)? When I first started, this is what day one looked like. I muscle tested: Is my weight set point 180? I received a "yes."

• Can I reset to 145? I received a no.
• Can I reset to 155? No again.
• Can I reset to 165? Another no.
• Can I reset to 175? Still no.
• Can I reset to 179? Finally, I got a yes.

I do this weekly. You can play around with this, do it daily, every other day, etc. See what is a fit for you. You can even ask. Can I reset in one day, two days, three days, etc.?

What about financial setpoints? This question varies from person to person and also depends on how you think about and measure your income. I work with salespeople who think in terms of weeks, months, quarters, or years.

One of my clients, Chris, who felt stuck at $325,000 a year, knew it was just a mind-set thing but could not push past the setpoint of this amount. After we released all of his unprocessed emotions and many sabotage beliefs around money, we reset to the next setpoint that he was open to embracing. Ultimately, $500,000 was the number. That week after the reset, Chris was offered a signing bonus of $175,000 to join a different brokerage.

When you think about your income, what is the first number that comes to mind? Imagine if you could shift your unseen financial blocks. You can. First, determine your financial setpoint (weekly, monthly, yearly) whatever is the most common way you think about your income.

Next through muscle testing determine your new setpoint. This is usually a stretch but not a strain and can increase incrementally. Notice how money flows to you in new ways. Unexpected money in the mail. New business opportunities. Owed money flows back to you. Celebrate every dollar as if it is a million. Get into the vibration of abundance. Shift your financial setpoint and shift your income.

There are endless categories of set points. Maybe you have a team of 100 people, and you would like a team of 1,000 or more. Maybe you would like to have additional income streams or need a certain amount of money to be debt-free. Maybe you want to sell above a certain number of units like books sold, or products bought. Maybe you have a certain setpoint with followers on your social media accounts. Check out the chart to be your guide but don't be afraid to set your own categories. The options are endless. Muscle test to see if you have a set point, then reset it.

WE'VE COVERED
THE PROCESS, NOW,

*are you ready?*

*let's begin!*

# Theme:
## CORE SKILLS

## EXERCISE 1: INTRODUCTION TO CORE SKILLS

*STOP* right this second, close your eyes and picture picture the journey complete! Picture yourself telling someone about how you showed up everyday and had transformational results. Imagine what it feels like to get out of your own way. How would your life be different? Write out your journey as if it is complete and you have achieved your goals.

## I STARTED MY JOURNEY BECAUSE I...

_____
_____
_____
_____
_____
_____
_____
_____

## AND NOW I AM...

_____
_____
_____
_____
_____
_____
_____
_____

Using the Alarm Method, answer this question: **What are you feeling right now about committing to this journey of transformational growth?**

**Awareness: What am I feeling?** (refer to index for list of emotions)

_____

_____

**Location: Where am I feeling it in my body?** (circle the area)

_____

_____

_____

**Ask yourself: When have I felt this before?** (Write any memories that pop up; notice them, don't judge. If nothing pops up, go to the next step.)

_____

_____

_____

_____

_____

_____

**Release: Allow the feeling to expand.** (Breathe in through your nose and out through your mouth 5-10 times. The emotion and all the thoughts attached to it releases like steam from a pot! It's that simple.)

**Mantra: What is the new emotion/statement you would like to replace the old one with?** (Use the packing method to pack this in.)

_____

_____

Use this space to write out any additional memories, thoughts, or emotions that came up while using the ALARM Method.

_____

_____

_____

_____

_____

_____

_____

_____

_____

_____

_____

_____

_____

_____

_____

_____

_____

_____

_____

_____

_____

_____

_____

_____

There are many ways to muscle test, everything from snapping your fingers, moving your hand across a surface, using a pendulum, and many more. The sway test (explained below) is my favorite for its simplicity, but feel free to search for the way that works best for you.

### Sway Test

Stand up tall with your feet pointing directly forward, hip-width apart. Make sure they're not turned slightly in or out.

Relax your body and keep your arms down by your side. Notice how you sway ever so slightly even as you stand still. To begin, you need to ask a foundational question to check for accuracy

Don't just read this.
## STAND UP! TRY THIS RIGHT NOW!

- Speak your correct name out loud. My name is _____.
- Now tune into the movement of your body.
- Speak a false name out loud. My name is _____.

Again, tune into the movement of your body. Think about it this way, you lean into and towards truth positivity, and you fall away from negativity and deceit. At this moment, look for which way your body sways. Now that you are tuned in to your body's movement, you can ask "yes/no" questions to continue using the sway test. Be mindful of the response of your body to each statement. You should feel yourself gently pulled forward for a correct response, a "yes" or pushed back indicating it's not true or your body is not in resonance with that, which would be a "no" response.

Your UPE Score is the amount of unprocessed emotions you have stuck in your body. The goal is to give you the skills to release these until your score is zero! How? Muscle test to see how many unprocessed emotions you have.

## TO DETERMINE YOUR UPE:

- Start by asking, "Do I have more than 250 unprocessed emotions?" (The average adult has around 250 so starting here makes sense.)
- If you get a no, then ask, "Do I have more than 100?"
- If you get a yes, then ask again, "Is it more than 150?"
- Continue to ask until you land on the number.
- I have seen scores as few as five and as many as 2500.
- This is a process of elimination, so work your way to your number.

I currently have

_____

unprocessed emotions!

## EXERCISE 5: RELEASE UPE'S WITH UNPACKING

The next step is to release your unprocessed emotions. Review the list of emotions to see if any of them are stuck somewhere in your body. Use my unpacking method to release the emotion. Then, use muscle testing to see if you cleared it or not. If you have, then use the packing method to replace the old beliefs with a new mantra.

## EMOTIONS

powerlessness
unworthiness
depression
insecurity
anxiety
despair
grief
shame
pride
worry
discouragement
disappointment
vulnerability
humiliation
unsupported
trauma/shock
jealousy
blame
anger
rage
unappreciated
overwhelm
frustration
irritation
impatience
pessimism
boredom
doubt
guilt

## OVERVIEW OF THE PROCESS:

- Use muscle testing to identify unprocessed emotions.
- Use the unpacking method to release what you find.
- Muscle test to see if the emotion was released (if not, repeat unpacking movement until cleared)

*You can also use the ALARM method to identify and release.

Use the space below to write about any emotions or stories that came up.

_____

_____

_____

_____

_____

_____

_____

_____

_____

_____

_____

_____

_____

_____

## EXERCISE 6: RELEASE SABOTAGE BELIEFS

Look at the following list of common sabotage beliefs and muscle test each belief, or use the ALARM Method if needed. If you are unsure of any, mark them as a "yes." If you are using muscle testing, you can test each statement with the question, "Do I have this sabotage belief?"

As you identify your sabotage beliefs, you can release them with the unpacking method. This is three sweeping movements, shoulder to wrist, on each arm. Include a new mantra that is the opposite of the sabotage belief you are releasing. For example, if the sabotage belief is, "I'll never be accepted." Unpack that with six sweeping movements. As a bonus, you can do the unpacking movement again and replace it with a new mantra, such as, "I am always accepted." Now, reset your filter to search for proof of what you want to see. In the example of, "I am accepted," you could grab a pen and paper and brainstorm all of the ways you are accepted. You want to reset your filter to notice and let in where you are accepted.

## COMMON SABOTAGE BELIEFS

I am worthless
I am ugly
The world is unsafe
I don't deserve love
I'll never be loved
I hate myself
I don't have control
I don't deserve forgiveness
I'm not worthy of respect
I'm stuck
I'm trapped
I destroy everything
I'm all alone
I'll never be accepted
I'm not enough
I'm broken/unfixable

There's not enough
There's not enough time
I'm an imposter
I'm dangerous
I'm out of control
I'm a mess
I'm stupid
Everything is dangerous/scary
I shouldn't exist
I don't belong
I'll never catch up/I'm behind
There's no point in trying
I never win
I'm not important
I'm too old
Growth is painful

Wealth is hard
Money is bad
I have to earn love
I'm weak
I'm not a priority
People will betray me
Making money is stressful
I can't have it all
If I shine, others get hurt
Other's needs are more
important than mine

## EXERCISE 6: RELEASE SABOTAGE BELIEFS CONT.

### SABOTAGE BELIEFS I CLEARED TODAY:

_____

_____

_____

_____

_____

_____

_____

_____

_____

### NEW MANTRAS I CAN SPEAK OUT & PACK IN:

_____

_____

_____

_____

_____

_____

_____

_____

_____

_____

## EXERCISE 7: WHAT DID I LEARN?

*What have I learned so far?*

_____
_____
_____
_____
_____

*What did I identify as the loudest emotions and limiting beliefs that are affecting how I show up daily?*

_____
_____
_____
_____
_____

*What am I looking forward to?*

_____
_____
_____
_____
_____

*It would be amazing if at the end of this journey I am...*

_____
_____
_____
_____
_____

# Great Job!
## LET'S MOVE TO THE NEXT SECTION.

# Theme:
## WEALTH

## EXERCISE 1: WHAT DID I DISCOVER?

Reflecting on financial experiences and decisions that have happened in the past can provide valuable insights into your current financial habits, beliefs, emotions, mindset and values. Here are some prompts that will help you mark the timeline up until now that have shaped your views and life around finances.

*It would be super powerful to answer a few of these questions and then go to the 15 Minute Daily Exercises to identify and release.* These prompts will activate old unprocessed emotions, raise to the surface sabotage beliefs and highlight set points to reset.

## EARLY INFLUENCES:

- What were your earliest memories of money?
- How did your family's financial situation shape your views on money?
- Were there any specific lessons or values related to money that were taught to you as a child? (money doesn't grow on trees, money causes unhappiness, you have to work hard for money, etc.)

---
---
---
---
---
---
---
---
---
---
---
---
---

## FINANCIAL MILESTONES:

- What were the most significant financial milestones in your life (e.g., first job, buying a home, paying off debt)?
- How did you feel when you reached these milestones?
- What challenges did you face, and if you overcame those challenges how did you do it?

_____
_____
_____
_____
_____
_____
_____
_____
_____
_____
_____
_____
_____
_____
_____
_____
_____
_____

## FINANCIAL MISTAKES & LESSONS LEARNED:

- Have you made any financial mistakes that had a lasting impact on your life?
- What did you learn from these mistakes?
- How have these lessons influenced your current financial behavior?

_____
_____
_____
_____
_____
_____
_____
_____
_____
_____

## VALUES AND BELIEFS:

- How do your personal values align with your financial decisions?
- Have your financial beliefs changed over time? If so, how and why?
- How do you define financial success? How close are you to achieving it?
- Do you believe it is okay to want money?

_____
_____
_____
_____
_____
_____
_____
_____
_____

## RELATIONSHIPS AND MONEY:

- How have your relationships influenced your financial decisions?
- Have you ever experienced conflict over money with family/friends?
- How were your parents around money?
- How do you feel about financial discussions with your partner/family members?

_____
_____
_____
_____
_____
_____
_____
_____
_____
_____
_____

## CAREER AND FINANCES:

- How has your career path influenced your financial situation?
- Have you ever made a career decision solely based on financial considerations? How did it turn out?
- What role does money play in your overall job satisfaction?

_____
_____
_____
_____
_____
_____

_____
_____
_____
_____
_____
_____
_____
_____

## EMOTIONS AND MONEY:

- How does your financial situation affect your emotional well-being?
- Have you ever made an emotional decision related to money? What was the outcome?
- How do you cope with financial stress or anxiety?
- How do you feel when you think of debt?
- How do you feel when you think of income?

_____
_____
_____
_____
_____
_____
_____
_____
_____
_____
_____

## FUTURE FINANCIAL GOALS:

- What are your financial goals for the future?
- What support or resources do you need to reach these goals?
- How do you feel about your financial goals?

Mark the time line with specific occurrences that impacted your past regarding finances, use the previous exercise to prompt your memory. Mark times along the timeline that impacted your thoughts/mindset/life around finances.

Use the future timeline to write in new achievements for your future self!

BIRTH      CURRENT AGE

├──────────────────────────────────────────────────┤

CURRENT AGE      FUTURE SELF

├──────────────────────────────────────────────────┤

## EXERCISE 3: WHAT I WANT / DON'T WANT

This exercise is powerful in that you get to say out loud what you want AND what you don't want. First, what DON'T YOU WANT regarding finances?

Now, what DO YOU WANT regarding finances? Make sure to write what you want in positive language in the bubble below!

After you have brainstormed ALL of the things you want and don't want, create a positive statement about what you want as if it is already happening. *Example: I am a great steward with my money. I am earning X amount monthly, all my bills are paid on time, my debt is paid in full. I have X amount in savings and I have more than enough money to do all the things I want to do.*

_____

_____

_____

This exercise is about redefining words that are important to your financial goals. One thing that was drilled into me when I started my personal growth journey was to only speak out the positive, never speak out the negative, and only say what you WANT. Recently, I learned from the author Tyler Watson, who wrote *The Alignment Effect*, that words can also be neutral. They become negatively or positively charged when spoken depending on YOUR associations with them.

The goal of this exercise is to redefine words so that they bring light and joy and attract what you want, versus bringing pain, triggers, and unwanted feelings. If you look at the previous exercise you can choose the words that hold a charge for you in that statement and define the ideal definitions and the non-ideal definitions.

For example, using this statement, we'll choose our words to redefine in **BOLD**:
I am a great **STEWARD** with my money. I am earning X amount monthly, all my bills are paid on time, my **DEBT** is paid in full. I have X amount in **SAVINGS** and I have more than enough **INCOME** to do all the things I want to do.

| Word to Redefine: DEBT | |
| --- | --- |
| **MY NON-IDEAL DEFINITION** | **MY IDEAL DEFINITION** |
| impossible to pay back | easy to pay back |
| keeps growing | use it to get what I want |
| makes me feel sick | empowers me |
| no control over it | completely my choice |
| out of control | helps me achieve my goals more quickly |
| weakens me | provides me a home |

Now, using your financial-related words that hold a charge for you, fill in the following tables to redefine your language and create ideal definitions.

| Word to Redefine: | |
|---|---|
| **MY NON-IDEAL DEFINITION** | **MY IDEAL DEFINITION** |
| | |
| | |
| | |
| | |
| | |
| | |

| Word to Redefine: | |
|---|---|
| **MY NON-IDEAL DEFINITION** | **MY IDEAL DEFINITION** |
| | |
| | |
| | |
| | |
| | |
| | |

| Word to Redefine: | |
|---|---|
| **MY NON-IDEAL DEFINITION** | **MY IDEAL DEFINITION** |
| | |
| | |
| | |
| | |
| | |
| | |

| Word to Redefine: | |
|---|---|
| **MY NON-IDEAL DEFINITION** | **MY IDEAL DEFINITION** |
| | |
| | |
| | |
| | |
| | |
| | |

The "Perfect Day" exercise is a powerful visualization which helps you get clear on what you want. Imagine, in vivid detail, what your perfect day would look like if there were no limitations or obstacles around finances. (You can do a variation of this called the Perfect Vacation Day, too! )

Find a quiet, comfortable space to relax close your eyes or find an object to gaze at. Take a few deep breaths in through the nose and out through the mouth. You will be picturing your perfect day from start to finish. Note the prompts which will help you do this. Once completed (you have gone to sleep in your perfect day), open your eyes and write it out.

Take note of anything that popped up for you as annoying, or what you didn't want or didn't feel "realistic". These are great clues to what still needs healing. For the moment, just notice and go back to what you want.

## PROMPTS TO GUIDE YOU:

- Wake up. What time is it? Where are you? Who are you with? What's the first thing you think/feel/do?
- What are you eating? Who are you spending time with? What are you feeling?
- How are you spending the evening?
- How do you wind down? What are your final thoughts before sleep?
- Include all five senses in your visualization. What do you see, hear, smell, taste, and feel throughout the day?
- Write it down in detail, review and say out loud daily or weekly, as you do this, notice if there are words to redefine in your story (words that evoke judgement, insecurity, anxiety or disbelief.)

_____

_____

_____

_____

_____

_____

## EXERCISE 6: I WANT A REWRITE!

Pick something that happened in the past that was less than ideal around finances and rewrite it the way you would have liked to have seen it happen. Rewrite old jobs, credit cards, forgotten bills, purchases, investments, anything that comes to mind!

_____

_____

_____

_____

_____

_____

_____

_____

_____

_____

_____

_____

_____

_____

_____

_____

_____

_____

_____

_____

_____

_____

## EXERCISE 7: THE MAGIC WAND

This is similar to the Perfect Day Exercise, but instead you imagine that you magically win 100 million dollars. What do you do? What do you spend the money on first? Who do you help? Where do you travel? Do you quit your job or buy a different home?

_____

_____

_____

_____

_____

_____

_____

_____

_____

_____

_____

_____

_____

_____

_____

_____

_____

_____

_____

_____

_____

_____

_____

_____

Affirmations are positive statements that can help individuals change their beliefs and attitudes toward money. Here's a list of powerful "I AM" affirmations related to money:

- I am financially abundant and secure.
- I make wise financial decisions with ease.
- Money flows to me easily and effortlessly.
- I am a magnet for wealth and prosperity.
- I am grateful for financial opportunities that come my way.
- I am a money-making machine, constantly creating new income streams.
- I am worthy of financial success and abundance.
- I am in control of my financial future and destiny.
- I am confident in my ability to manage and grow my wealth.
- I am open to receiving unexpected financial blessings.
- I am aligned with the energy of abundance and prosperity.
- I am constantly attracting opportunities to increase my wealth.
- I am financially free and live a life of financial independence.
- I am generous with my wealth and use it to positively impact others.
- I am content with my financial situation and trust that I have enough.
- I am constantly learning and growing in my financial knowledge and skills.
- I am at peace with money and see it as a tool for achieving my dreams.
- I am responsible with money and use it wisely.
- I am aligned with my financial goals and work towards them daily.
- I am grateful for all the wealth I have and excited for what's to come.

These affirmations can be used in daily practices, journaling, or meditation to help foster a positive and empowering relationship with money. By repeating and internalizing these statements, you can help shift your mindset toward abundance and financial success, aligning with abundance.

  TIP: If any of these statements create a negative response or resistance in you, do the Redefining Language exercise found on previous pages.

Use the lines below to write some of your own finance-related affirmations!

_____

_____

_____

_____

_____

_____

_____

_____

_____

_____

_____

_____

_____

_____

_____

_____

_____

_____

_____

_____

_____

_____

_____

_____

_____

## AFFIRMATION HACK: I WONDER...

If you speak out your affirmation and immediately feel what I call a "kickback" (the voice in your head that says, yeah right, followed by a sick feeling in the pit of your stomach), try this...

Let's say your affirmation is, "I am earning $50,000 per month." The dollar amount is whatever you want; it could be $5,000 or $500,000, it's up to you! Now instead of saying, "I am earning $50,000 a month," you say, "I wonder what it would feel like to earn $50,000 a month?" Your brain will search for the answer. Et voila! You are on your way to a new vibe!

## AFFIRMATION HACK: MIX IT UP

The main reason people get frustrated with affirmations is they feel like they are lying to themselves. One approach is to affirm what you already have, along with what you are wanting to attract. For example:

• I am grateful for my amazing closet that looks professionally organized! (That's one you don't have.)
• I am excited about the checks coming in the mail. (You already have this.)
• A steady job (You already have this.)
• I got the promotion at work (Looking forward to this.)
• I am worthy of love (isn't everyone?)
• I am powerful (deep down we all have untapped power.)
• I am courageous (maybe you haven't been yet, but...)

Merge what is with what could be, and watch your vibe change, then watch your life change!

*Bonus Power Up!*
Use the packing movement from the ALARM METHOD and speak out your affirmation. Have the intention that you are stepping into that new affirmation. Example: Say, "I am abundant," (three times) while sweeping down the arm from shoulder to wrist with the other hand. Then alternate. Do this 3-6 times.

## GRATITUDE HACK: RAISING HALLELUJAH

For the faith-filled individual, this is a power-packed daily routine. Include God in your gratitude. Using the acronym P.A.T.H., you can speak out your gratitude like so:

**P** **RAY**—heartfelt prayer declaring what is on your heart.

**A** **FFIRM**—affirmation that all is well and has come to fruition.

**T** **HANK**—giving gratitude for all you have and all that is coming.

**H** **ALLELUJAH/PRAISE**—praising God for all your blessings, answered prayers, and unanswered prayers.

Even if your beliefs do not exactly fit this exercise, spending time in reflection, affirming, thanking, and giving praise for all life has brought you, is incredibly powerful.

**P** RAY _____

_____

_____

**A** FFIRM _____

_____

_____

**T** HANK _____

_____

_____

**H** ALLELUJAH/PRAISE _____

_____

_____

## GRATITUDE HACK: WRITE IT OUT

Write out ten things you are grateful for each morning, then speak it out loud, then spend a few minutes reflecting on the things you are grateful for. You can also add in a gratitude walk and notice everything you are grateful for!

1 _____

2 _____

3 _____

4 _____

5 _____

6 _____

7 _____

8 _____

9 _____

10 _____

## GRATITUDE HACK: MESSAGES & BLESSINGS

Message one person daily for 30 days and tell them why you are grateful for them. Be authentic. Why are you grateful specifically for them? Really spend time thinking about how that person has blessed you. These can be people you have paid for services, your phone company, the bank teller, your book keeper, someone who is working hard at their own business, your partner, your children, etc. Be sure to schedule time for this into your calendar for 30 days!

## COLLECT PROOF OF YOUR SUCCESS

Proofing is one of my favourite exercises. This resets the filter settings we have programmed into place. Our minds are always looking for proof that we are right. If you speak out that you are broke all the time, your mind will search for ways you are broke. But if you program your mind to look for proof, you are RICH! You will see it, feel it, and create new opportunities of abundance. Ask yourself, how am I rich? Then write out all the ways you are RICH! Write into the cirlce what you are searching for proof of, then on the surrounding lines, write your PROOF that what's in the circle is true!

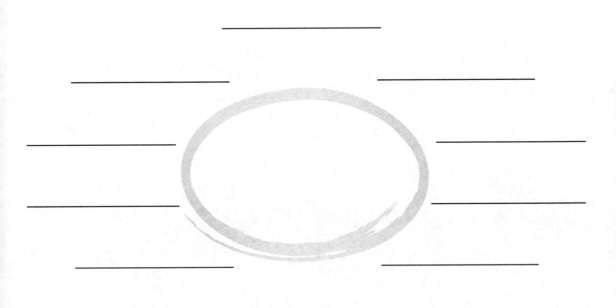

# Great Job!
## LET'S MOVE TO THE NEXT SECTION.

# Theme:
## HEALTH

## EXERCISE 1: WHAT DID I DISCOVER?

Reflecting on health experiences and decisions can provide valuable insights into your health habits, beliefs, and overall well-being. Here are some thoughtful prompts that can guide reflection in regard to health:

# EARLY INFLUENCES:
- What were your earliest memories of health and wellness?
- How did your family's attitudes and behaviors towards health shape your views?
- Were there any specific lessons or values related to health and well-being that were taught to you as a child?

_____

_____

_____

_____

_____

_____

_____

_____

_____

_____

_____

_____

_____

# HEALTH MILESTONES & CHALLENGES:
- What have been the most significant health milestones or challenges in your life?
- How did you feel when you reached or faced these milestones or challenges?
- What resources or support helped you through these times?

_____
_____
_____
_____
_____
_____
_____
_____
_____
_____
_____
_____
_____
_____
_____
_____
_____
_____

## DIET AND NUTRITION:

- How has your diet evolved over time?
- Have you ever tried specific diets or eating patterns? What were the outcomes?
- How do you feel about your current eating habits?

_____
_____
_____
_____
_____
_____

_____
_____
_____
_____
_____
_____
_____
_____
_____
_____

## EXERCISE AND PHYSICAL ACTIVITY:

- What role has exercise played in your life?
- Have you faced any barriers to maintaining a regular exercise routine? How did you overcome them?
- How do you feel about your current level of physical activity?

_____
_____
_____
_____
_____
_____
_____
_____
_____
_____

## MENTAL AND EMOTIONAL WELL-BEING:

- How do you take care of your mental and emotional health?
- Have you ever sought professional help for mental health concerns? What was that experience like?
- What practices or habits contribute to your emotional well-being?

_____

_____

_____

_____

_____

_____

_____

_____

_____

_____

_____

## RELATIONSHIPS AND HEALTH:

- How have your relationships influenced your health decisions?
- Have you ever experienced conflict over health-related issues with family or friends?
- How do you approach health-related discussions with your partner and family?

_____

_____

_____

_____

_____

_____
_____
_____
_____
_____
_____
_____
_____

## HEALTHCARE EXPERIENCES:

- What have been your experiences with healthcare providers and the healthcare system?
- Have you ever faced difficulties accessing healthcare? How did you navigate those challenges?
- How do you feel about your current healthcare providers and the care you receive?

_____
_____
_____
_____
_____
_____
_____
_____
_____
_____
_____

## WORK-LIFE BALANCE:

- How do you balance work and personal life to maintain your health?
- Have you ever felt that work negatively impacted your health? How did you address it?
- What strategies do you use to create a healthy work-life balance?

_____
_____
_____
_____
_____
_____
_____
_____
_____

## FUTURE HEALTH GOALS:

- Based on your past experiences, what are your health goals for the future?
- How are you planning to achieve these goals?
- What support or resources do you need to reach these goals?

_____
_____
_____
_____
_____
_____
_____
_____
_____

## EXERCISE 2: HEALTH TIMELINES

Mark the time line with specific occurrences that impacted your past regarding health, use the previous exercise to prompt your memory. Mark times along the timeline that impacted your thoughts/mindset/life around health.

Use the future timeline to write in new achievements for your future healthy self!

BIRTH                                                    CURRENT AGE
├─────────────────────────────────────────────────────┤

CURRENT AGE                                              FUTURE SELF
├─────────────────────────────────────────────────────┤

## EXERCISE 3: WHAT I WANT / DON'T WANT

This exercise is powerful in that you get to say out loud what you want AND what you don't want. First, what DON'T YOU WANT regarding health?

Now, what DO YOU WANT regarding health? Make sure to write what you want in positive language in the bubble below!

After you have brainstormed ALL of the things you want and don't want, create a positive statement about what you want as if it is already happening. *Example: I am my ideal weight, I have amazing energy and feel confident in my health. I look and feel younger than my years. I am strong and every cell in my body is miraculously healthy.*

This exercise is about redefining words that are important to your health goals. One thing that was drilled into me when I started my personal growth journey was to only speak out the positive, never speak out the negative, and only say what you WANT. Recently, I learned from the author Tyler Watson, who wrote *The Alignment Effect*, that words can also be neutral. They become negatively or positively charged when spoken depending on YOUR associations with them.

The goal of this exercise is to redefine words so that they bring light and joy and attract what you want, versus bringing pain, triggers, and unwanted feelings. If you look at the previous exercise you can choose the words that hold a charge for you in that statement and define the ideal definitions and the non-ideal definitions.

For example, using this statement, we'll choose our words to redefine in **BOLD**:
I am my **IDEAL WEIGHT**, I have amazing **ENERGY** and feel confident in my health. I look and feel younger than my years. I am **STRONG** and every cell in my body is miraculously **HEALTHY**.

| Word to Redefine: IDEAL WEIGHT ||
| :---: | :---: |
| **MY NON-IDEAL DEFINITION** | **MY IDEAL DEFINITION** |
| feels impossible | easy to hit this goal |
| I keep gaining | I love being healthy |
| I can't lose | I love how my clothes feel |
| no control over it | I choose my weight |
| out of control | I feel happy |
| not going to happen | I love feeling young |

Now, using your health-related words that hold a charge for you, fill in the following tables to redefine your language and create ideal definitions.

| Word to Redefine: | |
| --- | --- |
| **MY NON-IDEAL DEFINITION** | **MY IDEAL DEFINITION** |
| | |
| | |
| | |
| | |
| | |
| | |

| Word to Redefine: | |
| --- | --- |
| **MY NON-IDEAL DEFINITION** | **MY IDEAL DEFINITION** |
| | |
| | |
| | |
| | |
| | |
| | |

| Word to Redefine: | |
|---|---|
| **MY NON-IDEAL DEFINITION** | **MY IDEAL DEFINITION** |
| | |
| | |
| | |
| | |
| | |
| | |

| Word to Redefine: | |
|---|---|
| **MY NON-IDEAL DEFINITION** | **MY IDEAL DEFINITION** |
| | |
| | |
| | |
| | |
| | |
| | |

## EXERCISE 5: THE PERFECT DAY

The "Perfect Day" exercise is a powerful visualization which helps you get clear on what you want. Imagine, in vivid detail, what your perfect day would look like if there were no limitations or obstacles around health. (You can do a variation of this called the Perfect Vacation Day, too! )

Find a quiet, comfortable space to relax close your eyes or find an object to gaze at. Take a few deep breaths in through the nose and out through the mouth. You will be picturing your perfect day from start to finish. Note the prompts which will help you do this. Once completed (you have gone to sleep in your perfect day), open your eyes and write it out.

Take note of anything that popped up for you as annoying, or what you didn't want or didn't feel "realistic". These are great clues to what still needs healing. For the moment, just notice and go back to what you want.

## PROMPTS TO GUIDE YOU:
- Wake up. What time is it? Where are you? Who are you with? What's the first thing you think/feel/do?
- What are you eating? Who are you spending time with? What are you feeling?
- How are you spending the evening?
- How do you wind down? What are your final thoughts before sleep?
- Include all five senses in your visualization. What do you see, hear, smell, taste, and feel throughout the day?
- Write it down in detail, review and say out loud daily or weekly, as you do this, notice if there are words to redefine in your story (words that evoke judgement, insecurity, anxiety or disbelief.)

_____

_____

_____

_____

_____

_____

Pick something that happened in the past that was less than ideal around health and rewrite it the way you would have liked to have seen it happen. Rewrite accidents, sicknesses, energy, weight gain or loss, eating habits, anything that comes to mind!

_____

_____

_____

_____

_____

_____

_____

_____

_____

_____

_____

_____

_____

_____

_____

_____

_____

_____

_____

_____

_____

_____

_____

## EXERCISE 7: THE MAGIC WAND

This is similar to the Perfect Day Exercise, but instead you imagine that you are instantly in perfect health. What do you do? What would you do differently? How would you wake up? Who would you call? Where do you travel? How would life be different?

# EXERCISE 8: POWERFUL AFFIRMATIONS

Affirmations are positive statements that can help individuals change their beliefs and attitudes toward health. Here's a list of powerful "I AM" affirmations related to health:

- I am in perfect health and full of vitality.
- I am grateful for my strong and healthy body.
- I am in control of my health and wellness.
- I am nourishing my body with healthy food and positive thoughts.
- I am constantly healing and rejuvenating.
- I am active and energetic, embracing physical activity with joy.
- I am at peace with my body and accept it fully.
- I am committed to taking care of myself and prioritizing my well-being.
- I am resilient and overcome health challenges with grace.
- I am in tune with my body's needs and respond with love and care.
- I am free from stress and cultivate inner peace.
- I am focused on positive thoughts that enhance my health.
- I am confident in my body's ability to heal and thrive.
- I am embracing a balanced and healthy lifestyle.
- I am radiating health, happiness, and well-being.

These affirmations can be used in daily practices, journaling, or meditation to help foster a positive and empowering relationship with your health. By repeating and internalizing these statements, you can help shift your mindset toward health and aligning with health/wellness.

 TIP: If any of these statements create a negative response or resistance in you, do the Redefining Language exercise found on previous pages.

## EXERCISE 8: POWERFUL AFFIRMATIONS CONT.

Use the lines below to write some of your own health-related affirmations!

## AFFIRMATION HACK: I WONDER...

If you speak out your affirmation and immediately feel what I call a "kickback" (the voice in your head that says, yeah right, followed by a sick feeling in the pit of your stomach), try this...

Let's say your affirmation is, "I am full of energy and passion!" Now instead of saying, that you say, "I wonder what it would feel like to be full of energy and passion?" Your brain will search for the answer. Et voila! You are on your way to a new vibe!

## AFFIRMATION HACK: MIX IT UP

The main reason people get frustrated with affirmations is they feel like they are lying to themselves. One approach is to affirm what you already have, along with what you want to attract. For example:

• I am grateful for my amazing closet that looks professionally organized! (That's one you don't have.)
• I am excited about the checks coming in the mail. (You already have this.)
• A steady job (You already have this.)
• I got the promotion at work (Looking forward to this.)
• I am worthy of love (isn't everyone?)
• I am powerful (deep down we all have untapped power.)
• I am courageous (maybe you haven't been yet, but...)

Merge what is with what could be, and watch your vibe change, then watch your life change!

*Bonus Power Up!*
Use the packing movement from the ALARM METHOD and speak out your affirmation. Have the intention that you are stepping into that new affirmation. Example: Say, "I am healthy," (three times) while sweeping down the arm from shoulder to wrist with the other hand. Then alternate. Do this 3-6 times.

## GRATITUDE HACK: RAISING HALLELUJAH

For the faith-filled individual, this is a power-packed daily routine. Include God in your gratitude. Using the acronym P.A.T.H., you can speak out your gratitude like so:

**P** **RAY** —heartfelt prayer declaring what is on your heart.

**A** **FFIRM** —affirmation that all is well and has come to fruition.

**T** **HANK** —giving gratitude for all you have and all that is coming.

**H** **ALLELUJAH/PRAISE** —praising God for all your blessings, answered prayers, and unanswered prayers.

Even if your beliefs do not exactly fit this exercise, spending time in reflection, affirming, thanking, and giving praise for all life has brought you, is incredibly powerful.

**P** **RAY** _____

_____

_____

**A** **FFIRM** _____

_____

_____

**T** **HANK** _____

_____

_____

**H** **ALLELUJAH/PRAISE** _____

_____

_____

## GRATITUDE HACK: WRITE IT OUT

Write out ten things you are grateful for each morning, then speak it out loud, then spend a few minutes reflecting on the things you are grateful for. You can also add in a gratitude walk and notice everything you are grateful for!

1 _____
_____

2 _____
_____

3 _____
_____

4 _____
_____

5 _____
_____

6 _____
_____

7 _____
_____

8 _____
_____

9 _____
_____

10 _____
_____

## GRATITUDE HACK: MESSAGES TO YOUR BODY

For 30 days write out one bodily function or body part or system that you are grateful for. Why are you grateful specifically for them? Really spend time thinking about this. How are you blessed in the health department? Be sure to schedule time for this into your calendar for 30 days!

## COLLECT PROOF OF YOUR SUCCESS

Proofing is one of my favourite exercises. This resets the filter settings we have programmed into place. Our minds are always looking for proof that we are right. If you speak out that you are sick all the time, your mind will search for ways you are sick, where there is pain, discomfort, malfunction, and illness. But if you program your mind to look for proof, you are HEALTHY! You will see it, feel it, and create new opportunities for health. Ask yourself, how am I healthy? Then write out all the ways you are HEALTHY! Write into the cirlce what you are searching for proof of, then on the surrounding lines, write your PROOF that what's in the circle is true!

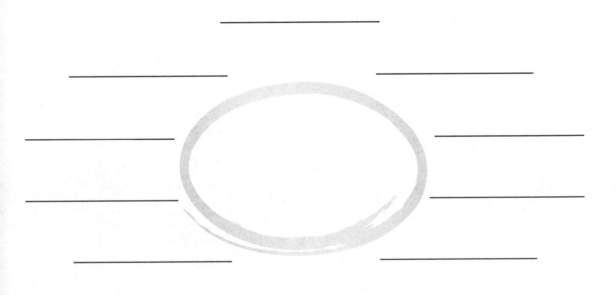

# Great Job!

## LET'S MOVE TO THE NEXT SECTION.

## Theme:
### RELATIONSHIPS

## EXERCISE 1: WHAT DID I DISCOVER?

Relationships ( this can represent friendships, significant other, or family) Use the example that is "loudest" or most pressing as you work through the following exercises. Reflecting on relationship experiences and decisions can provide valuable insights into an individual's interpersonal habits, beliefs, and overall connection with others. Here are some thoughtful prompts that can guide reflection in regard to relationships:

# EARLY INFLUENCES:

- What were your earliest memories of relationships and connections with others?
- How did your family's attitudes and behaviors towards relationships shape your views?
- Were there any specific lessons or values related to relationships taught to you as a child?

_____
_____
_____
_____
_____
_____
_____
_____
_____
_____
_____
_____
_____
_____
_____
_____

## SIGNIFICANT RELATIONSHIPS:

- Who have been the most significant people in your life, and why?
- What have been the most meaningful relationships in your life, whether romantic, familial, or platonic?
- How have these relationships shaped who you are today?

_____
_____
_____
_____
_____
_____
_____
_____
_____
_____
_____
_____
_____
_____
_____
_____
_____
_____

## CHALLENGES AND CONFLICTS:

- What have been the most challenging relationships in your life?
- How have you handled conflicts within relationships?
- What have you learned from these challenges and conflicts?

_____
_____
_____
_____
_____
_____
_____
_____
_____
_____

## COMMUNICATION AND BOUNDARIES:

- How do you communicate your needs and feelings within relationships?
- How do you set and maintain boundaries with others?
- Have you ever struggled with communication or boundaries? How did you address those struggles?

_____
_____
_____
_____
_____
_____
_____
_____
_____
_____

## LOVE AND ROMANCE

- How do you approach romantic relationships?
- What have been your most significant romantic relationships, and what did you learn from them?
- How do you define love, and how has that definition evolved over time?

_____

_____

_____

_____

_____

_____

_____

_____

_____

_____

## FRIENDSHIP

- How do you cultivate and maintain friendships?
- What qualities do you value most in friends?
- Have you ever faced challenges in friendships? How did you navigate those challenges?

_____

_____

_____

_____

_____

_____

_____
_____
_____
_____
_____

## FAMILY RELATIONSHIPS:

- How would you describe your relationships with family members?
- Have you ever faced conflicts or challenges within your family? How did you handle them?
- How have family relationships influenced your views on relationships in general?

_____
_____
_____
_____
_____
_____
_____
_____

## WORK RELATIONSHIPS

- How do you approach relationships with colleagues and superiors at work?
- Have you ever faced challenges in work relationships? How did you address them?
- How do you balance professional and personal relationships?

_____
_____
_____
_____
_____

_____

_____

_____

_____

_____

## SELF-RELATIONSHIP

- How do you view your relationship with yourself?
- What practices or habits contribute to a positive self-relationship?
- How do you nurture self-love and self-acceptance?

_____

_____

_____

_____

_____

_____

_____

## FUTURE RELATIONSHIP GOALS

- Based on your past experiences, what are your relationship goals for the future?

_____

_____

_____

_____

_____

_____

_____

Mark the time line with specific occurrences that impacted your past regarding relationships, use the previous exercise to prompt your memory. Mark times along the timeline that impacted your thoughts/mindset/life around relationships.

Use the future timeline to write in new achievements for your future self!

BIRTH                                                          CURRENT AGE

CURRENT AGE                                                    FUTURE SELF

## EXERCISE 3: WHAT I WANT / DON'T WANT

This exercise is powerful in that you get to say out loud what you want AND what you don't want. First, what DON'T YOU WANT regarding relationships?

Now, what DO YOU WANT regarding relationships? Make sure to write what you want in positive language in the bubble below!

After you have brainstormed ALL of the things you want and don't want, create a positive statement about what you want as if it is already happening. *Example: I enjoy a healthy relationship with my extended family with kind boundaries in place. I love my husband and laugh with him often, we have lots of adventures together and still feel in love and excited to hang out. My kids come to me for advice and feel supported. My friendships lift me up and are encouraging. I feel supported and loved.*

_____

_____

_____

# EXERCISE 4: REDEFINING LANGUAGE

This exercise is about redefining words that are important to your relationship goals. One thing that was drilled into me when I started my personal growth journey was to only speak out the positive, never speak out the negative, and only say what you WANT. Recently, I learned from the author Tyler Watson, who wrote *The Alignment Effect*, that words can also be neutral. They become negatively or positively charged when spoken depending on YOUR associations with them.

The goal of this exercise is to redefine words so that they bring light and joy and attract what you want, versus bringing pain, triggers, and unwanted feelings. If you look at the previous exercise you can choose the words that hold a charge for you in that statement and define the ideal definitions and the non-ideal definitions.

For example, using this statement, we'll choose our words to redefine in **BOLD**:
I enjoy a healthy **RELATIONSHIP** with my **EXTENDED FAMILY** with kind **BOUNDARIES** in place. I love my husband and laugh with him often, we have lots of adventures together and still feel in love and excited to hang out. My kids come to me for advice and feel supported. My **FRIENDSHIPS** lift me up and are encouraging. I feel supported and loved.

| Word to Redefine: FRIENDSHIPS ||
| MY NON-IDEAL DEFINITION | MY IDEAL DEFINITION |
| --- | --- |
| dont' feel support | feel supported |
| feel misunderstood | love connecting |
| worried about hurting feelings | excited to share good news |
| feel judged | my friends hold space for me |
| dont feel safe being vulnerable | safe to be vulnerable |
| secretly undermining/distrust | feel encouraged/trust |

Now, using your relationship-related words that hold a charge for you, fill in the following tables to redefine your language and create ideal definitions.

| Word to Redefine: | |
|---|---|
| **MY NON-IDEAL DEFINITION** | **MY IDEAL DEFINITION** |
| | |
| | |
| | |
| | |
| | |
| | |

| Word to Redefine: | |
|---|---|
| **MY NON-IDEAL DEFINITION** | **MY IDEAL DEFINITION** |
| | |
| | |
| | |
| | |
| | |
| | |

| Word to Redefine: | |
|---|---|
| **MY NON-IDEAL DEFINITION** | **MY IDEAL DEFINITION** |
| | |
| | |
| | |
| | |
| | |
| | |

| Word to Redefine: | |
|---|---|
| **MY NON-IDEAL DEFINITION** | **MY IDEAL DEFINITION** |
| | |
| | |
| | |
| | |
| | |
| | |

## EXERCISE 5: THE PERFECT DAY

The "Perfect Day" exercise is a powerful visualization which helps you get clear on what you want. Imagine, in vivid detail, what your perfect day would look like if there were no limitations or obstacles around relationships. (You can do a variation of this called the Perfect Vacation Day, too! )

Find a quiet, comfortable space to relax close your eyes or find an object to gaze at. Take a few deep breaths in through the nose and out through the mouth. You will be picturing your perfect day from start to finish. Note the prompts which will help you do this. Once completed (you have gone to sleep in your perfect day), open your eyes and write it out.

Take note of anything that popped up for you as annoying, or what you didn't want or didn't feel "realistic". These are great clues to what still needs healing. For the moment, just notice and go back to what you want.

## PROMPTS TO GUIDE YOU:

- Wake up. What time is it? Where are you? Who are you with? What's the first thing you think/feel/do?
- What are you eating? Who are you spending time with? What are you feeling?
- How are you spending the evening?
- How do you wind down? What are your final thoughts before sleep?
- Include all five senses in your visualization. What do you see, hear, smell, taste, and feel throughout the day?
- Write it down in detail, review and say out loud daily or weekly, as you do this, notice if there are words to redefine in your story (words that evoke judgement, insecurity, anxiety or disbelief.)

_____

_____

_____

_____

_____

_____

# EXERCISE 6: I WANT A REWRITE!

Pick something that happened in the past that was less than ideal around relationships and rewrite it the way you would have liked to have seen it happen. Rewrite friendships, family members, upbringing, significant others, anything that comes to mind!

_____
_____
_____
_____
_____
_____
_____
_____
_____
_____
_____
_____
_____
_____
_____
_____
_____
_____
_____
_____
_____
_____

## EXERCISE 7: THE MAGIC WAND

This is similar to the Perfect Day Exercise, but instead you imagine that you magically wake up to the perfect significant other relationship, or friendship, or family (whatever is most pressing to you.) What do you do? Who or what is different? Who do you call? How do they treat you? How do you feel about them?

_____
_____
_____
_____
_____
_____
_____
_____
_____
_____
_____
_____
_____
_____
_____
_____
_____
_____
_____
_____
_____
_____
_____

# EXERCISE 8: POWERFUL AFFIRMATIONS

Affirmations are positive statements that can help individuals change their beliefs and attitudes toward relationships. Here's a list of powerful "I AM" affirmations related to relationships:

- I am worthy of love and connection.
- I am open to giving and receiving love fully.
- I am building strong and meaningful relationships.
- I am a compassionate and understanding partner.
- I am attracting positive and loving people into my life.
- I am respectful and valued in my relationships.
- I am committed to clear and honest communication.
- I am nurturing /supportive to those I love.
- I am growing and evolving through my relationships.
- I am forgiving and let go of past hurts.
- I am confident in my ability to create healthy boundaries.
- I am grateful for the love and support I receive from others.
- I am joyful and find happiness in my connections with others.
- I am a loyal friend and partner, building trust in my relationships.
- I am embracing love in all its forms and expressions.

These affirmations can be used in daily practices, journaling, or meditation to help foster a positive and empowering relationship with your relationships. By repeating and internalizing these statements, you can help shift your mindset toward relationships and aligning with healthy, fulfilling relationships.

 TIP: If any of these statements create a negative response or resistance in you, do the Redefining Language exercise found on previous pages.

## EXERCISE 8: POWERFUL AFFIRMATIONS CONT.

Use the lines below to write some of your own relationship-related affirmations!

_____

_____

_____

_____

_____

_____

_____

_____

_____

_____

_____

_____

_____

_____

_____

_____

_____

_____

_____

_____

_____

_____

_____

_____

## AFFIRMATION HACK: I WONDER...

If you speak out your affirmation and immediately feel what I call a "kickback" (the voice in your head that says, yeah right, followed by a sick feeling in the pit of your stomach), try this...

Let's say your affirmation is, "I am in a happy marriage," but it doesn't resonate with you. Try " I wonder what a happy marriage feels like" Your brain will search for the answer. Et voila! You are on your way to a new vibe!

## AFFIRMATION HACK: MIX IT UP

The main reason people get frustrated with affirmations is they feel like they are lying to themselves. One approach is to affirm what you already have, along with what you want to attract. For example:

• I am grateful for my amazing closet that looks professionally organized! (That's one you don't have.)
• I am excited about the checks coming in the mail. (You already have this.)
• A steady job (You already have this.)
• I got the promotion at work (Looking forward to this.)
• I am worthy of love (isn't everyone?)
• I am powerful (deep down we all have untapped power.)
• I am courageous (maybe you haven't been yet, but...)

Merge what is with what could be, and watch your vibe change, then watch your life change!

***Bonus Power Up!***
Use the packing movement from the ALARM METHOD and speak out your affirmation. Have the intention that you are stepping into that new affirmation. Example: Say, "I am loved and supported," (three times) while sweeping down the arm from shoulder to wrist with the other hand. Then alternate. Do this 3-6 times.

## GRATITUDE HACK: RAISING HALLELUJAH

For the faith-filled individual, this is a power-packed daily routine. Include God in your gratitude. Using the acronym P.A.T.H., you can speak out your gratitude like so:

**P RAY** —heartfelt prayer declaring what is on your heart.

**A FFIRM** —affirmation that all is well and has come to fruition.

**T HANK** —giving gratitude for all you have and all that is coming.

**H ALLELUJAH/PRAISE** —praising God for all your blessings, answered prayers, and unanswered prayers.

Even if your beliefs do not exactly fit this exercise, spending time in reflection, affirming, thanking, and giving praise for all life has brought you, is incredibly powerful.

**P RAY** _____

_____

_____

**A FFIRM** _____

_____

_____

**T HANK** _____

_____

_____

**H ALLELUJAH/PRAISE** _____

_____

_____

## GRATITUDE HACK: WRITE IT OUT

Write out ten things you are grateful for each morning, then speak it out loud, then spend a few minutes reflecting on the things you are grateful for. You can also add in a gratitude walk and notice everything you are grateful for!

1 _____

2 _____

3 _____

4 _____

5 _____

6 _____

7 _____

8 _____

9 _____

10 _____

## GRATITUDE HACK: MESSAGES TO YOUR BODY

Message one new person a for 30 days and tell them why you are grateful for them in your life. Be authentic. Why are you grateful specifically for them? Really spend time thinking about how that person has blessed you. Get excited each day to pick a new person. Be sure to schedule time for this into your calendar for 30 days!

## COLLECT PROOF OF YOUR SUCCESS

Proofing is one of my favourite exercises. This resets the filter settings we have programmed into place. Our minds are always looking for proof that we are right. If you speak out that people hurt you all the time or don't hear you, or you are not respected or you can't trust people, your mind will search for ways you are right. You will only notice when you get hurt, tricked, disrespected, etc. But if you program your mind to look for proof that you are respected, who does hear you? Who CAN you trust? You will see it, feel it, and create new opportunities for powerful relationships and attract more into your life. Ask yourself, who respects me? Then write out all the ways you are RESEPCTED! Write into the cirlce what you are searching for proof of, then on the surrounding lines, write your PROOF that what's in the circle is true!

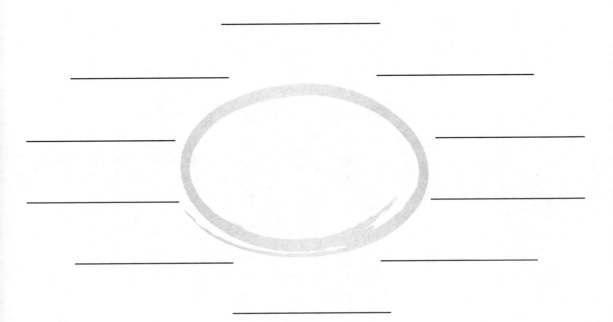

# Your Daily
## 15 MINUTE
## EMOTIONAL RESET

# EXAMPLE: DAILY 15 MIN. EMOTIONAL RESET

When I first started doing this work, it took approximately 15 to 30 minutes a day of releasing over a three month period to release many of the emotions and sabotage beliefs that were holding me back. I wasn't able to release each and every day, but I did do exercises which helped raise my vibration and assisted me in moving into action steps to achieve my dreams and goals. The purpose of this 15 minute a day exercise is to help you do the same... Step into your divine mission and shine brightest!

**DATE:** Oct. 4, 2023          **THEME:** Monthly Income

*How do you feel about your theme on a scale of 1-10?* _____4_____

*What's your current UPE Score?* _____203_____

*Loudest Emotions cleared today?*
anxiety (identify and unpack)

*Limiting Beliefs cleared today?*
there's never enough time (identify and unpack)

*Old Set Point?*
$3000 monthly

*Reset to New Set Point?*
$4500 monthly

*New Mantra to pack in?*
I have supernatural time to get everything done!

*Reflections on what I identified, released, and reset today...*
I have anxiety about how much time I have per month to make enough to pay the bills. My new mantra helps me feel more relaxed about getting everything done. I was surprised anxiety came up and am happy to release it.

*My new story (written in the present) is...*
I'm so excited that I increased my income and that I have more than enough time to get everything done in the month!

**DATE:** **THEME:**

How do you feel about your theme
on a scale of 1-10? _____

What's your current UPE Score?

_____

Loudest Emotions cleared today?

_____

Sabotaging Beliefs cleared today?

_____

Old Set Point?

_____ /99

Reset to New Set Point?

_____ /99

New Mantra to pack in?

_____

Reflections on what I identified, released, and reset today...

_____
_____
_____

My new story (written in the present) is...

_____
_____

---

**DATE:** **THEME:**

How do you feel about your theme
on a scale of 1-10? _____

What's your current UPE Score?

_____

Loudest Emotions cleared today?

_____

Sabotaging Beliefs cleared today?

_____

Old Set Point?

_____ /99

Reset to New Set Point?

_____ /99

New Mantra to pack in?

_____

Reflections on what I identified, released, and reset today...

_____
_____
_____

My new story (written in the present) is...

_____
_____

**DATE:**                              **THEME:**

How do you feel about your theme
on a scale of 1-10? _____

What's your current UPE Score?

_____

Loudest Emotions cleared today?

_____

Sabotaging Beliefs cleared today?

_____

Old Set Point?

_____ /99

Reset to New Set Point?

_____ /99

New Mantra to pack in?

_____

Reflections on what I identified, released, and reset today...

_____
_____
_____

My new story (written in the present) is...

_____
_____


**DATE:**                              **THEME:**

How do you feel about your theme
on a scale of 1-10? _____

What's your current UPE Score?

_____

Loudest Emotions cleared today?

_____

Sabotaging Beliefs cleared today?

_____

Old Set Point?

_____ /99

Reset to New Set Point?

_____ /99

New Mantra to pack in?

_____

Reflections on what I identified, released, and reset today...

_____
_____
_____

My new story (written in the present) is...

_____
_____

**DATE:**                          **THEME:**

How do you feel about your theme
on a scale of 1-10? _____

What's your current UPE Score?

_____

Loudest Emotions cleared today?

_____

Sabotaging Beliefs cleared today?

_____

Old Set Point?

_____ /99

Reset to New Set Point?

_____ /99

New Mantra to pack in?

_____

Reflections on what I identified, released, and reset today...

_____
_____
_____

My new story (written in the present) is...

_____
_____

---

**DATE:**                          **THEME:**

How do you feel about your theme
on a scale of 1-10? _____

What's your current UPE Score?

_____

Loudest Emotions cleared today?

_____

Sabotaging Beliefs cleared today?

_____

Old Set Point?

_____ /99

Reset to New Set Point?

_____ /99

New Mantra to pack in?

_____

Reflections on what I identified, released, and reset today...

_____
_____
_____

My new story (written in the present) is...

_____
_____

**DATE:**                    **THEME:**

How do you feel about your theme
on a scale of 1-10? _____

What's your current UPE Score?

_____

Loudest Emotions cleared today?

_____

Sabotaging Beliefs cleared today?

_____

Old Set Point?

_____ /99

Reset to New Set Point?

_____ /99

New Mantra to pack in?

_____

Reflections on what I identified, released, and reset today...

_____

_____

_____

My new story (written in the present) is...

_____

_____

_____

**DATE:**                    **THEME:**

How do you feel about your theme
on a scale of 1-10? _____

What's your current UPE Score?

_____

Loudest Emotions cleared today?

_____

Sabotaging Beliefs cleared today?

_____

Old Set Point?

_____ /99

Reset to New Set Point?

_____ /99

New Mantra to pack in?

_____

Reflections on what I identified, released, and reset today...

_____

_____

_____

My new story (written in the present) is...

_____

_____

**DATE:**             **THEME:**

How do you feel about your theme on a scale of 1-10? _____

What's your current UPE Score? _____

Loudest Emotions cleared today?
_____

Sabotaging Beliefs cleared today?
_____

Old Set Point?
_____ /99

Reset to New Set Point?
_____ /99

New Mantra to pack in?
_____

Reflections on what I identified, released, and reset today...
_____
_____
_____

My new story (written in the present) is...
_____
_____
_____

---

**DATE:**             **THEME:**

How do you feel about your theme on a scale of 1-10? _____

What's your current UPE Score? _____

Loudest Emotions cleared today?
_____

Sabotaging Beliefs cleared today?
_____

Old Set Point?
_____ /99

Reset to New Set Point?
_____ /99

New Mantra to pack in?
_____

Reflections on what I identified, released, and reset today...
_____
_____
_____

My new story (written in the present) is...
_____
_____

**DATE:**                **THEME:**

How do you feel about your theme
on a scale of 1-10? _____

What's your current UPE Score?

_____

Loudest Emotions cleared today?

_____

Sabotaging Beliefs cleared today?

_____

Old Set Point?

_____ /99

Reset to New Set Point?

_____ /99

New Mantra to pack in?

_____

Reflections on what I identified, released, and reset today...

_____

_____

_____

My new story (written in the present) is...

_____

_____


**DATE:**                **THEME:**

How do you feel about your theme
on a scale of 1-10? _____

What's your current UPE Score?

_____

Loudest Emotions cleared today?

_____

Sabotaging Beliefs cleared today?

_____

Old Set Point?

_____ /99

Reset to New Set Point?

_____ /99

New Mantra to pack in?

_____

Reflections on what I identified, released, and reset today...

_____

_____

_____

My new story (written in the present) is...

_____

_____

**DATE:**                                    **THEME:**

How do you feel about your theme
on a scale of 1-10? _____

What's your current UPE Score?

_____

Loudest Emotions cleared today?

_____

Sabotaging Beliefs cleared today?

_____

Old Set Point?

_____ /99

Reset to New Set Point?

_____ /99

New Mantra to pack in?

_____

Reflections on what I identified, released, and reset today...

_____

_____

_____

My new story (written in the present) is...

_____

_____

_____


**DATE:**                                    **THEME:**

How do you feel about your theme
on a scale of 1-10? _____

What's your current UPE Score?

_____

Loudest Emotions cleared today?

_____

Sabotaging Beliefs cleared today?

_____

Old Set Point?

_____ /99

Reset to New Set Point?

_____ /99

New Mantra to pack in?

_____

Reflections on what I identified, released, and reset today...

_____

_____

_____

My new story (written in the present) is...

_____

_____

_____

**DATE:**                   **THEME:**

How do you feel about your theme
on a scale of 1-10? _____

What's your current UPE Score?

_____

Loudest Emotions cleared today?

_____

Sabotaging Beliefs cleared today?

_____

Old Set Point?

_____ /99

Reset to New Set Point?

_____ /99

New Mantra to pack in?

_____

Reflections on what I identified, released, and reset today...

_____

_____

_____

My new story (written in the present) is...

_____

_____

---

**DATE:**                   **THEME:**

How do you feel about your theme
on a scale of 1-10? _____

What's your current UPE Score?

_____

Loudest Emotions cleared today?

_____

Sabotaging Beliefs cleared today?

_____

Old Set Point?

_____ /99

Reset to New Set Point?

_____ /99

New Mantra to pack in?

_____

Reflections on what I identified, released, and reset today...

_____

_____

_____

My new story (written in the present) is...

_____

_____

**DATE:**                                  **THEME:**

How do you feel about your theme
on a scale of 1-10? _____

What's your current UPE Score?

_____

Loudest Emotions cleared today?

Sabotaging Beliefs cleared today?

_____

_____

Old Set Point?

Reset to New Set Point?

_____ /99

_____ /99

New Mantra to pack in?

_____

Reflections on what I identified, released, and reset today...

_____

_____

_____

My new story (written in the present) is...

_____

_____


**DATE:**                                  **THEME:**

How do you feel about your theme
on a scale of 1-10? _____

What's your current UPE Score?

_____

Loudest Emotions cleared today?

Sabotaging Beliefs cleared today?

_____

_____

Old Set Point?

Reset to New Set Point?

_____ /99

_____ /99

New Mantra to pack in?

_____

Reflections on what I identified, released, and reset today...

_____

_____

_____

My new story (written in the present) is...

_____

_____

**DATE:**           **THEME:**

How do you feel about your theme
on a scale of 1-10? _____

What's your current UPE Score?

_____

Loudest Emotions cleared today?

_____

Sabotaging Beliefs cleared today?

_____

Old Set Point?

_____ /99

Reset to New Set Point?

_____ /99

New Mantra to pack in?

_____

Reflections on what I identified, released, and reset today...

_____

_____

_____

My new story (written in the present) is...

_____

_____


**DATE:**           **THEME:**

How do you feel about your theme
on a scale of 1-10? _____

What's your current UPE Score?

_____

Loudest Emotions cleared today?

_____

Sabotaging Beliefs cleared today?

_____

Old Set Point?

_____ /99

Reset to New Set Point?

_____ /99

New Mantra to pack in?

_____

Reflections on what I identified, released, and reset today...

_____

_____

_____

My new story (written in the present) is...

_____

_____

**DATE:**                **THEME:**

How do you feel about your theme
on a scale of 1-10? _____

What's your current UPE Score?

_____

Loudest Emotions cleared today?

_____

Sabotaging Beliefs cleared today?

_____

Old Set Point?

_____ /99

Reset to New Set Point?

_____ /99

New Mantra to pack in?

_____

Reflections on what I identified, released, and reset today...

_____
_____
_____

My new story (written in the present) is...

_____
_____

---

**DATE:**                **THEME:**

How do you feel about your theme
on a scale of 1-10? _____

What's your current UPE Score?

_____

Loudest Emotions cleared today?

_____

Sabotaging Beliefs cleared today?

_____

Old Set Point?

_____ /99

Reset to New Set Point?

_____ /99

New Mantra to pack in?

_____

Reflections on what I identified, released, and reset today...

_____
_____
_____

My new story (written in the present) is...

_____
_____

**DATE:**             **THEME:**

How do you feel about your theme
on a scale of 1-10? _____

What's your current UPE Score?

_____

Loudest Emotions cleared today?

_____

Sabotaging Beliefs cleared today?

_____

Old Set Point?

_____ /99

Reset to New Set Point?

_____ /99

New Mantra to pack in?

_____

Reflections on what I identified, released, and reset today...

_____

_____

_____

My new story (written in the present) is...

_____

_____

---

**DATE:**             **THEME:**

How do you feel about your theme
on a scale of 1-10? _____

What's your current UPE Score?

_____

Loudest Emotions cleared today?

_____

Sabotaging Beliefs cleared today?

_____

Old Set Point?

_____ /99

Reset to New Set Point?

_____ /99

New Mantra to pack in?

_____

Reflections on what I identified, released, and reset today...

_____

_____

_____

My new story (written in the present) is...

_____

_____

**DATE:**  **THEME:**

How do you feel about your theme
on a scale of 1-10?  _____

What's your current UPE Score?

_____

Loudest Emotions cleared today?

Sabotaging Beliefs cleared today?

_____

_____

Old Set Point?

Reset to New Set Point?

_____ /99

_____ /99

New Mantra to pack in?

_____

Reflections on what I identified, released, and reset today...

_____

_____

_____

My new story (written in the present) is...

_____

_____


**DATE:**  **THEME:**

How do you feel about your theme
on a scale of 1-10?  _____

What's your current UPE Score?

_____

Loudest Emotions cleared today?

Sabotaging Beliefs cleared today?

_____

_____

Old Set Point?

Reset to New Set Point?

_____ /99

_____ /99

New Mantra to pack in?

_____

Reflections on what I identified, released, and reset today...

_____

_____

_____

My new story (written in the present) is...

_____

_____

**DATE:**                              **THEME:**

How do you feel about your theme
on a scale of 1-10? _____

What's your current UPE Score?

_____

Loudest Emotions cleared today?

Sabotaging Beliefs cleared today?

_____

_____

Old Set Point?

Reset to New Set Point?

_____ /99

_____ /99

New Mantra to pack in?

_____

Reflections on what I identified, released, and reset today...

_____

_____

_____

My new story (written in the present) is...

_____

_____

_____


**DATE:**                              **THEME:**

How do you feel about your theme
on a scale of 1-10? _____

What's your current UPE Score?

_____

Loudest Emotions cleared today?

Sabotaging Beliefs cleared today?

_____

_____

Old Set Point?

Reset to New Set Point?

_____ /99

_____ /99

New Mantra to pack in?

_____

Reflections on what I identified, released, and reset today...

_____

_____

_____

My new story (written in the present) is...

_____

_____

**DATE:** _____          **THEME:** _____

How do you feel about your theme
on a scale of 1-10? _____

What's your current UPE Score?

_____

Loudest Emotions cleared today?

_____

Sabotaging Beliefs cleared today?

_____

Old Set Point?

_____ /99

Reset to New Set Point?

_____ /99

New Mantra to pack in?

_____

Reflections on what I identified, released, and reset today...

_____

_____

_____

My new story (written in the present) is...

_____

_____


**DATE:** _____          **THEME:** _____

How do you feel about your theme
on a scale of 1-10? _____

What's your current UPE Score?

_____

Loudest Emotions cleared today?

_____

Sabotaging Beliefs cleared today?

_____

Old Set Point?

_____ /99

Reset to New Set Point?

_____ /99

New Mantra to pack in?

_____

Reflections on what I identified, released, and reset today...

_____

_____

_____

My new story (written in the present) is...

_____

_____

**DATE:**                         **THEME:**

*How do you feel about your theme*          *What's your current UPE Score?*
*on a scale of 1-10?* _____          _____

*Loudest Emotions cleared today?*          *Sabotaging Beliefs cleared today?*
_____          _____

*Old Set Point?*                          *Reset to New Set Point?*
_____ /99                      _____ /99

*New Mantra to pack in?*

_____

*Reflections on what I identified, released, and reset today...*

_____
_____
_____

*My new story (written in the present) is...*

_____
_____

---

**DATE:**                         **THEME:**

*How do you feel about your theme*          *What's your current UPE Score?*
*on a scale of 1-10?* _____          _____

*Loudest Emotions cleared today?*          *Sabotaging Beliefs cleared today?*
_____          _____

*Old Set Point?*                          *Reset to New Set Point?*
_____ /99                      _____ /99

*New Mantra to pack in?*

_____

*Reflections on what I identified, released, and reset today...*

_____
_____
_____

*My new story (written in the present) is...*

_____
_____

**DATE:**                     **THEME:**

How do you feel about your theme
on a scale of 1-10? _____

What's your current UPE Score?

_____

Loudest Emotions cleared today?

_____

Sabotaging Beliefs cleared today?

_____

Old Set Point?

_____ /99

Reset to New Set Point?

_____ /99

New Mantra to pack in?

_____

Reflections on what I identified, released, and reset today...

_____
_____
_____

My new story (written in the present) is...

_____
_____

---

**DATE:**                     **THEME:**

How do you feel about your theme
on a scale of 1-10? _____

What's your current UPE Score?

_____

Loudest Emotions cleared today?

_____

Sabotaging Beliefs cleared today?

_____

Old Set Point?

_____ /99

Reset to New Set Point?

_____ /99

New Mantra to pack in?

_____

Reflections on what I identified, released, and reset today...

_____
_____
_____

My new story (written in the present) is...

_____
_____

**DATE:**                                **THEME:**

How do you feel about your theme
on a scale of 1-10? _____

What's your current UPE Score?

_____

Loudest Emotions cleared today?

_____

Sabotaging Beliefs cleared today?

_____

Old Set Point?

_____ /99

Reset to New Set Point?

_____ /99

New Mantra to pack in?

_____

Reflections on what I identified, released, and reset today...

_____

_____

_____

My new story (written in the present) is...

_____

_____

_____


**DATE:**                                **THEME:**

How do you feel about your theme
on a scale of 1-10? _____

What's your current UPE Score?

_____

Loudest Emotions cleared today?

_____

Sabotaging Beliefs cleared today?

_____

Old Set Point?

_____ /99

Reset to New Set Point?

_____ /99

New Mantra to pack in?

_____

Reflections on what I identified, released, and reset today...

_____

_____

_____

My new story (written in the present) is...

_____

_____

_____

**DATE:**          **THEME:**

How do you feel about your theme
on a scale of 1-10? _____

What's your current UPE Score?
_____

Loudest Emotions cleared today?
_____

Sabotaging Beliefs cleared today?
_____

Old Set Point?
_____ /99

Reset to New Set Point?
_____ /99

New Mantra to pack in?
_____

Reflections on what I identified, released, and reset today...
_____
_____
_____

My new story (written in the present) is...
_____
_____


**DATE:**          **THEME:**

How do you feel about your theme
on a scale of 1-10? _____

What's your current UPE Score?
_____

Loudest Emotions cleared today?
_____

Sabotaging Beliefs cleared today?
_____

Old Set Point?
_____ /99

Reset to New Set Point?
_____ /99

New Mantra to pack in?
_____

Reflections on what I identified, released, and reset today...
_____
_____
_____

My new story (written in the present) is...
_____
_____

**DATE:**   **THEME:**

How do you feel about your theme on a scale of 1-10? _____

What's your current UPE Score? _____

Loudest Emotions cleared today?
_____

Sabotaging Beliefs cleared today?
_____

Old Set Point?
_____ /99

Reset to New Set Point?
_____ /99

New Mantra to pack in?
_____

Reflections on what I identified, released, and reset today...
_____
_____
_____

My new story (written in the present) is...
_____
_____
_____

**DATE:**   **THEME:**

How do you feel about your theme on a scale of 1-10? _____

What's your current UPE Score? _____

Loudest Emotions cleared today?
_____

Sabotaging Beliefs cleared today?
_____

Old Set Point?
_____ /99

Reset to New Set Point?
_____ /99

New Mantra to pack in?
_____

Reflections on what I identified, released, and reset today...
_____
_____
_____

My new story (written in the present) is...
_____
_____

**DATE:**           **THEME:**

How do you feel about your theme on a scale of 1-10? _____

What's your current UPE Score? _____

Loudest Emotions cleared today?
_____

Sabotaging Beliefs cleared today?
_____

Old Set Point?
_____ /99

Reset to New Set Point?
_____ /99

New Mantra to pack in?

_____

Reflections on what I identified, released, and reset today...

_____

_____

_____

My new story (written in the present) is...

_____

_____

---

**DATE:**           **THEME:**

How do you feel about your theme on a scale of 1-10? _____

What's your current UPE Score? _____

Loudest Emotions cleared today?
_____

Sabotaging Beliefs cleared today?
_____

Old Set Point?
_____ /99

Reset to New Set Point?
_____ /99

New Mantra to pack in?

_____

Reflections on what I identified, released, and reset today...

_____

_____

_____

My new story (written in the present) is...

_____

_____

**DATE:**                    **THEME:**

How do you feel about your theme
on a scale of 1-10? _____

What's your current UPE Score?

_____

Loudest Emotions cleared today?

_____

Sabotaging Beliefs cleared today?

_____

Old Set Point?

_____ /99

Reset to New Set Point?

_____ /99

New Mantra to pack in?

_____

Reflections on what I identified, released, and reset today...

_____
_____
_____

My new story (written in the present) is...

_____
_____


**DATE:**                    **THEME:**

How do you feel about your theme
on a scale of 1-10? _____

What's your current UPE Score?

_____

Loudest Emotions cleared today?

_____

Sabotaging Beliefs cleared today?

_____

Old Set Point?

_____ /99

Reset to New Set Point?

_____ /99

New Mantra to pack in?

_____

Reflections on what I identified, released, and reset today...

_____
_____
_____

My new story (written in the present) is...

_____
_____

**DATE:**            **THEME:**

How do you feel about your theme
on a scale of 1-10? _____

What's your current UPE Score?

_____

Loudest Emotions cleared today?

_____

Sabotaging Beliefs cleared today?

_____

Old Set Point?

_____ /99

Reset to New Set Point?

_____ /99

New Mantra to pack in?

_____

Reflections on what I identified, released, and reset today...

_____
_____
_____

My new story (written in the present) is...

_____
_____

---

**DATE:**            **THEME:**

How do you feel about your theme
on a scale of 1-10? _____

What's your current UPE Score?

_____

Loudest Emotions cleared today?

_____

Sabotaging Beliefs cleared today?

_____

Old Set Point?

_____ /99

Reset to New Set Point?

_____ /99

New Mantra to pack in?

_____

Reflections on what I identified, released, and reset today...

_____
_____
_____

My new story (written in the present) is...

_____
_____

**DATE:**　　　　　　　　**THEME:**

How do you feel about your theme on a scale of 1-10? _____

What's your current UPE Score? _____

Loudest Emotions cleared today?

_____

Sabotaging Beliefs cleared today?

_____

Old Set Point?

_____ /99

Reset to New Set Point?

_____ /99

New Mantra to pack in?

_____

Reflections on what I identified, released, and reset today...

_____

_____

_____

My new story (written in the present) is...

_____

_____

---

**DATE:**　　　　　　　　**THEME:**

How do you feel about your theme on a scale of 1-10? _____

What's your current UPE Score? _____

Loudest Emotions cleared today?

_____

Sabotaging Beliefs cleared today?

_____

Old Set Point?

_____ /99

Reset to New Set Point?

_____ /99

New Mantra to pack in?

_____

Reflections on what I identified, released, and reset today...

_____

_____

My new story (written in the present) is...

_____

_____

**DATE:**           **THEME:**

How do you feel about your theme on a scale of 1-10? _____

What's your current UPE Score?

_____

Loudest Emotions cleared today?

_____

Sabotaging Beliefs cleared today?

_____

Old Set Point?

_____ /99

Reset to New Set Point?

_____ /99

New Mantra to pack in?

_____

Reflections on what I identified, released, and reset today...

_____

_____

_____

My new story (written in the present) is...

_____

_____

---

**DATE:**           **THEME:**

How do you feel about your theme on a scale of 1-10? _____

What's your current UPE Score?

_____

Loudest Emotions cleared today?

_____

Sabotaging Beliefs cleared today?

_____

Old Set Point?

_____ /99

Reset to New Set Point?

_____ /99

New Mantra to pack in?

_____

Reflections on what I identified, released, and reset today...

_____

_____

_____

My new story (written in the present) is...

_____

_____

**DATE:**                    **THEME:**

How do you feel about your theme
on a scale of 1-10? _____

What's your current UPE Score?

_____

Loudest Emotions cleared today?

_____

Sabotaging Beliefs cleared today?

_____

Old Set Point?

_____ /99

Reset to New Set Point?

_____ /99

New Mantra to pack in?

_____

Reflections on what I identified, released, and reset today...

_____
_____
_____

My new story (written in the present) is...

_____
_____


**DATE:**                    **THEME:**

How do you feel about your theme
on a scale of 1-10? _____

What's your current UPE Score?

_____

Loudest Emotions cleared today?

_____

Sabotaging Beliefs cleared today?

_____

Old Set Point?

_____ /99

Reset to New Set Point?

_____ /99

New Mantra to pack in?

_____

Reflections on what I identified, released, and reset today...

_____
_____
_____

My new story (written in the present) is...

_____
_____

**DATE:** _____  **THEME:** _____

How do you feel about your theme
on a scale of 1-10? _____

What's your current UPE Score?

_____

Loudest Emotions cleared today?

_____

Sabotaging Beliefs cleared today?

_____

Old Set Point?

_____ /99

Reset to New Set Point?

_____ /99

New Mantra to pack in?

_____

Reflections on what I identified, released, and reset today...

_____
_____
_____

My new story (written in the present) is...

_____
_____


**DATE:** _____  **THEME:** _____

How do you feel about your theme
on a scale of 1-10? _____

What's your current UPE Score?

_____

Loudest Emotions cleared today?

_____

Sabotaging Beliefs cleared today?

_____

Old Set Point?

_____ /99

Reset to New Set Point?

_____ /99

New Mantra to pack in?

_____

Reflections on what I identified, released, and reset today...

_____
_____
_____

My new story (written in the present) is...

_____
_____

**DATE:**　　　　　　　　**THEME:**

How do you feel about your theme
on a scale of 1-10? _____

What's your current UPE Score?

_____

Loudest Emotions cleared today?

_____

Sabotaging Beliefs cleared today?

_____

Old Set Point?

_____ /99

Reset to New Set Point?

_____ /99

New Mantra to pack in?

_____

Reflections on what I identified, released, and reset today...

_____

_____

_____

My new story (written in the present) is...

_____

_____


**DATE:**　　　　　　　　**THEME:**

How do you feel about your theme
on a scale of 1-10? _____

What's your current UPE Score?

_____

Loudest Emotions cleared today?

_____

Sabotaging Beliefs cleared today?

_____

Old Set Point?

_____ /99

Reset to New Set Point?

_____ /99

New Mantra to pack in?

_____

Reflections on what I identified, released, and reset today...

_____

_____

_____

My new story (written in the present) is...

_____

_____

**DATE:** _____  **THEME:** _____

How do you feel about your theme
on a scale of 1-10? _____

What's your current UPE Score?

_____

Loudest Emotions cleared today?

_____

Sabotaging Beliefs cleared today?

_____

Old Set Point?

_____ /99

Reset to New Set Point?

_____ /99

New Mantra to pack in?

_____

Reflections on what I identified, released, and reset today...

_____

_____

_____

My new story (written in the present) is...

_____

_____

_____

**DATE:** _____  **THEME:** _____

How do you feel about your theme
on a scale of 1-10? _____

What's your current UPE Score?

_____

Loudest Emotions cleared today?

_____

Sabotaging Beliefs cleared today?

_____

Old Set Point?

_____ /99

Reset to New Set Point?

_____ /99

New Mantra to pack in?

_____

Reflections on what I identified, released, and reset today...

_____

_____

_____

My new story (written in the present) is...

_____

_____

_____

**DATE:** _____     **THEME:** _____

How do you feel about your theme
on a scale of 1-10? _____

What's your current UPE Score?

_____

Loudest Emotions cleared today?

_____

Sabotaging Beliefs cleared today?

_____

Old Set Point?

_____ /99

Reset to New Set Point?

_____ /99

New Mantra to pack in?

_____

Reflections on what I identified, released, and reset today...

_____
_____
_____

My new story (written in the present) is...

_____
_____


**DATE:** _____     **THEME:** _____

How do you feel about your theme
on a scale of 1-10? _____

What's your current UPE Score?

_____

Loudest Emotions cleared today?

_____

Sabotaging Beliefs cleared today?

_____

Old Set Point?

_____ /99

Reset to New Set Point?

_____ /99

New Mantra to pack in?

_____

Reflections on what I identified, released, and reset today...

_____
_____
_____

My new story (written in the present) is...

_____
_____

**DATE:**           **THEME:**

How do you feel about your theme
on a scale of 1-10? _____

What's your current UPE Score?

_____

Loudest Emotions cleared today?

_____

Sabotaging Beliefs cleared today?

_____

Old Set Point?

_____ /99

Reset to New Set Point?

_____ /99

New Mantra to pack in?

_____

Reflections on what I identified, released, and reset today...

_____

_____

_____

My new story (written in the present) is...

_____

_____


**DATE:**           **THEME:**

How do you feel about your theme
on a scale of 1-10? _____

What's your current UPE Score?

_____

Loudest Emotions cleared today?

_____

Sabotaging Beliefs cleared today?

_____

Old Set Point?

_____ /99

Reset to New Set Point?

_____ /99

New Mantra to pack in?

_____

Reflections on what I identified, released, and reset today...

_____

_____

_____

My new story (written in the present) is...

_____

_____

**DATE:**                    **THEME:**

How do you feel about your theme
on a scale of 1-10? _____

What's your current UPE Score?
_____

Loudest Emotions cleared today?
_____

Sabotaging Beliefs cleared today?
_____

Old Set Point?
_____ /99

Reset to New Set Point?
_____ /99

New Mantra to pack in?

_____

Reflections on what I identified, released, and reset today...

_____
_____
_____

My new story (written in the present) is...

_____
_____


**DATE:**                    **THEME:**

How do you feel about your theme
on a scale of 1-10? _____

What's your current UPE Score?
_____

Loudest Emotions cleared today?
_____

Sabotaging Beliefs cleared today?
_____

Old Set Point?
_____ /99

Reset to New Set Point?
_____ /99

New Mantra to pack in?

_____

Reflections on what I identified, released, and reset today...

_____
_____
_____

My new story (written in the present) is...

_____
_____

**DATE:**                 **THEME:**

How do you feel about your theme
on a scale of 1-10? _____

What's your current UPE Score?

_____

Loudest Emotions cleared today?

_____

Sabotaging Beliefs cleared today?

_____

Old Set Point?

_____ /99

Reset to New Set Point?

_____ /99

New Mantra to pack in?

_____

Reflections on what I identified, released, and reset today...

_____

_____

_____

My new story (written in the present) is...

_____

_____


**DATE:**                 **THEME:**

How do you feel about your theme
on a scale of 1-10? _____

What's your current UPE Score?

_____

Loudest Emotions cleared today?

_____

Sabotaging Beliefs cleared today?

_____

Old Set Point?

_____ /99

Reset to New Set Point?

_____ /99

New Mantra to pack in?

_____

Reflections on what I identified, released, and reset today...

_____

_____

_____

My new story (written in the present) is...

_____

_____

**DATE:**                    **THEME:**

How do you feel about your theme
on a scale of 1-10? _____

What's your current UPE Score?

_____

Loudest Emotions cleared today?

_____

Sabotaging Beliefs cleared today?

_____

Old Set Point?

_____ /99

Reset to New Set Point?

_____ /99

New Mantra to pack in?

_____

Reflections on what I identified, released, and reset today...

_____

_____

_____

My new story (written in the present) is...

_____

_____


**DATE:**                    **THEME:**

How do you feel about your theme
on a scale of 1-10? _____

What's your current UPE Score?

_____

Loudest Emotions cleared today?

_____

Sabotaging Beliefs cleared today?

_____

Old Set Point?

_____ /99

Reset to New Set Point?

_____ /99

New Mantra to pack in?

_____

Reflections on what I identified, released, and reset today...

_____

_____

_____

My new story (written in the present) is...

_____

_____

**DATE:** _____   **THEME:** _____

How do you feel about your theme
on a scale of 1-10? _____

What's your current UPE Score?

_____

Loudest Emotions cleared today?

_____

Sabotaging Beliefs cleared today?

_____

Old Set Point?

_____ /99

Reset to New Set Point?

_____ /99

New Mantra to pack in?

_____

Reflections on what I identified, released, and reset today...

_____
_____
_____

My new story (written in the present) is...

_____
_____
_____


**DATE:** _____   **THEME:** _____

How do you feel about your theme
on a scale of 1-10? _____

What's your current UPE Score?

_____

Loudest Emotions cleared today?

_____

Sabotaging Beliefs cleared today?

_____

Old Set Point?

_____ /99

Reset to New Set Point?

_____ /99

New Mantra to pack in?

_____

Reflections on what I identified, released, and reset today...

_____
_____
_____

My new story (written in the present) is...

_____
_____

**DATE:**              **THEME:**

How do you feel about your theme
on a scale of 1-10? _____

What's your current UPE Score?

_____

Loudest Emotions cleared today?

_____

Sabotaging Beliefs cleared today?

_____

Old Set Point?

_____ /99

Reset to New Set Point?

_____ /99

New Mantra to pack in?

_____

Reflections on what I identified, released, and reset today...

_____

_____

_____

My new story (written in the present) is...

_____

_____

**DATE:**              **THEME:**

How do you feel about your theme
on a scale of 1-10? _____

What's your current UPE Score?

_____

Loudest Emotions cleared today?

_____

Sabotaging Beliefs cleared today?

_____

Old Set Point?

_____ /99

Reset to New Set Point?

_____ /99

New Mantra to pack in?

_____

Reflections on what I identified, released, and reset today...

_____

_____

_____

My new story (written in the present) is...

_____

_____

**DATE:**　　　　　　　　　**THEME:**

How do you feel about your theme
on a scale of 1-10? _____

What's your current UPE Score?

_____

Loudest Emotions cleared today?

_____

Sabotaging Beliefs cleared today?

_____

Old Set Point?

_____ /99

Reset to New Set Point?

_____ /99

New Mantra to pack in?

_____

Reflections on what I identified, released, and reset today...

_____
_____
_____

My new story (written in the present) is...

_____
_____


**DATE:**　　　　　　　　　**THEME:**

How do you feel about your theme
on a scale of 1-10? _____

What's your current UPE Score?

_____

Loudest Emotions cleared today?

_____

Sabotaging Beliefs cleared today?

_____

Old Set Point?

_____ /99

Reset to New Set Point?

_____ /99

New Mantra to pack in?

_____

Reflections on what I identified, released, and reset today...

_____
_____
_____

My new story (written in the present) is...

_____
_____

**DATE:**                           **THEME:**

How do you feel about your theme
on a scale of 1-10? _____

What's your current UPE Score?

_____

Loudest Emotions cleared today?

Sabotaging Beliefs cleared today?

_____

_____

Old Set Point?

Reset to New Set Point?

_____ /99

_____ /99

New Mantra to pack in?

_____

Reflections on what I identified, released, and reset today...

_____

_____

_____

My new story (written in the present) is...

_____

_____

---

**DATE:**                           **THEME:**

How do you feel about your theme
on a scale of 1-10? _____

What's your current UPE Score?

_____

Loudest Emotions cleared today?

Sabotaging Beliefs cleared today?

_____

_____

Old Set Point?

Reset to New Set Point?

_____ /99

_____ /99

New Mantra to pack in?

_____

Reflections on what I identified, released, and reset today...

_____

_____

_____

My new story (written in the present) is...

_____

_____

**DATE:**                  **THEME:**

How do you feel about your theme
on a scale of 1-10? _____

What's your current UPE Score?

_____

Loudest Emotions cleared today?

_____

Sabotaging Beliefs cleared today?

_____

Old Set Point?

_____ /99

Reset to New Set Point?

_____ /99

New Mantra to pack in?

_____

Reflections on what I identified, released, and reset today...

_____
_____
_____

My new story (written in the present) is...

_____
_____

---

**DATE:**                  **THEME:**

How do you feel about your theme
on a scale of 1-10? _____

What's your current UPE Score?

_____

Loudest Emotions cleared today?

_____

Sabotaging Beliefs cleared today?

_____

Old Set Point?

_____ /99

Reset to New Set Point?

_____ /99

New Mantra to pack in?

_____

Reflections on what I identified, released, and reset today...

_____
_____
_____

My new story (written in the present) is...

_____
_____

**DATE:** _____ **THEME:** _____

How do you feel about your theme
on a scale of 1-10? _____

What's your current UPE Score?
_____

Loudest Emotions cleared today?
_____

Sabotaging Beliefs cleared today?
_____

Old Set Point?
_____ /99

Reset to New Set Point?
_____ /99

New Mantra to pack in?

_____

Reflections on what I identified, released, and reset today...

_____
_____
_____

My new story (written in the present) is...

_____
_____


**DATE:** _____ **THEME:** _____

How do you feel about your theme
on a scale of 1-10? _____

What's your current UPE Score?
_____

Loudest Emotions cleared today?
_____

Sabotaging Beliefs cleared today?
_____

Old Set Point?
_____ /99

Reset to New Set Point?
_____ /99

New Mantra to pack in?

_____

Reflections on what I identified, released, and reset today...

_____
_____
_____

My new story (written in the present) is...

_____
_____

**DATE:** _____     **THEME:** _____

How do you feel about your theme
on a scale of 1-10? _____

What's your current UPE Score?

_____

Loudest Emotions cleared today?

_____

Sabotaging Beliefs cleared today?

_____

Old Set Point?

_____ /99

Reset to New Set Point?

_____ /99

New Mantra to pack in?

_____

Reflections on what I identified, released, and reset today...

_____

_____

_____

My new story (written in the present) is...

_____

_____

_____


**DATE:** _____     **THEME:** _____

How do you feel about your theme
on a scale of 1-10? _____

What's your current UPE Score?

_____

Loudest Emotions cleared today?

_____

Sabotaging Beliefs cleared today?

_____

Old Set Point?

_____ /99

Reset to New Set Point?

_____ /99

New Mantra to pack in?

_____

Reflections on what I identified, released, and reset today...

_____

_____

_____

My new story (written in the present) is...

_____

_____

**DATE:**                  **THEME:**

How do you feel about your theme
on a scale of 1-10? _____

What's your current UPE Score?

_____

Loudest Emotions cleared today?

Sabotaging Beliefs cleared today?

_____

_____

Old Set Point?

Reset to New Set Point?

_____ /99

_____ /99

New Mantra to pack in?

_____

Reflections on what I identified, released, and reset today...

_____

_____

_____

My new story (written in the present) is...

_____

_____

_____

**DATE:**                  **THEME:**

How do you feel about your theme
on a scale of 1-10? _____

What's your current UPE Score?

_____

Loudest Emotions cleared today?

Sabotaging Beliefs cleared today?

_____

_____

Old Set Point?

Reset to New Set Point?

_____ /99

_____ /99

New Mantra to pack in?

_____

Reflections on what I identified, released, and reset today...

_____

_____

_____

My new story (written in the present) is...

_____

_____

_____

## DATE:

## THEME:

How do you feel about your theme
on a scale of 1-10? _____

What's your current UPE Score?

_____

Loudest Emotions cleared today?

_____

Sabotaging Beliefs cleared today?

_____

Old Set Point?

_____ /99

Reset to New Set Point?

_____ /99

New Mantra to pack in?

_____

Reflections on what I identified, released, and reset today...

_____

_____

_____

My new story (written in the present) is...

_____

_____

## DATE:

## THEME:

How do you feel about your theme
on a scale of 1-10? _____

What's your current UPE Score?

_____

Loudest Emotions cleared today?

_____

Sabotaging Beliefs cleared today?

_____

Old Set Point?

_____ /99

Reset to New Set Point?

_____ /99

New Mantra to pack in?

_____

Reflections on what I identified, released, and reset today...

_____

_____

_____

My new story (written in the present) is...

_____

_____

**DATE:**                    **THEME:**

How do you feel about your theme
on a scale of 1-10? _____

What's your current UPE Score?

_____

Loudest Emotions cleared today?

_____

Sabotaging Beliefs cleared today?

_____

Old Set Point?

_____ /99

Reset to New Set Point?

_____ /99

New Mantra to pack in?

_____

Reflections on what I identified, released, and reset today...

_____

_____

_____

My new story (written in the present) is...

_____

_____


**DATE:**                    **THEME:**

How do you feel about your theme
on a scale of 1-10? _____

What's your current UPE Score?

_____

Loudest Emotions cleared today?

_____

Sabotaging Beliefs cleared today?

_____

Old Set Point?

_____ /99

Reset to New Set Point?

_____ /99

New Mantra to pack in?

_____

Reflections on what I identified, released, and reset today...

_____

_____

_____

My new story (written in the present) is...

_____

_____

**DATE:**            **THEME:**

How do you feel about your theme
on a scale of 1-10? _____

What's your current UPE Score?

_____

Loudest Emotions cleared today?

_____

Sabotaging Beliefs cleared today?

_____

Old Set Point?

_____ /99

Reset to New Set Point?

_____ /99

New Mantra to pack in?

_____

Reflections on what I identified, released, and reset today...

_____

_____

_____

My new story (written in the present) is...

_____

_____

_____

**DATE:**            **THEME:**

How do you feel about your theme
on a scale of 1-10? _____

What's your current UPE Score?

_____

Loudest Emotions cleared today?

_____

Sabotaging Beliefs cleared today?

_____

Old Set Point?

_____ /99

Reset to New Set Point?

_____ /99

New Mantra to pack in?

_____

Reflections on what I identified, released, and reset today...

_____

_____

_____

My new story (written in the present) is...

_____

_____

Made in United States
Troutdale, OR
10/31/2024

24335142R00095